Rocky Mountain Wildflowers

PHOTOS, DESCRIPTIONS, AND EARLY EXPLORER INSIGHTS

Jerry Pavia

D0027656

Fulcrum Publishing
Golden, Colorado

Library of Congress Cataloging-in-Publication Data

Pavia, Jerry.
Rocky mountain wildflowers : photos, descriptions,
& early explorer insights / Jerry Pavia.
        p. cm.
Includes bibliographical references and index.
    ISBN 1-55591-364-4 (pbk. : alk. paper)
1. Wildflowers—Rocky Mountains—Identification.
2. Wildflowers—Rocky Mountains—Pictorial works.
3. Mountain plants—Rocky Mountains—Identification.
4. Mountain plants—Rocky Mountains—Pictorial works.
I. Title.
QK139.P36 2003
582.13'0978—dc21

                                                    2002151234

                    Printed in China
                0 9 8 7 6 5 4 3 2 1

*Half of the royalties from this book will be donated to the Idaho Conservation League,
a nonprofit organization that works to protect and restore the water, wildlands,
and wildlife of Idaho through citizen action, public education, and professional advocacy.
You can learn more about the Idaho Conservation League's work at www.wildidaho.org.*

Editorial: Marlene Blessing, Ellen Wheat,
Daniel Forrest-Bank, Michele Wynn
Design: Constance Bollen, cb graphics
Front cover photograph: Beargrass (*Xerophyllum tenax*)
Back cover photographs (from left to right): trillium (*Trillium ovatum*),
salsify (*Tragopogon dubius*), Lewis's monkeyflower (*Mimulus lewisii*)

Fulcrum Publishing
16100 Table Mountain Parkway, Suite 300
Golden, Colorado 80403
(800) 992-2908 • (303) 277-1623
www.fulcrum-books.com

THIS BOOK IS DEDICATED TO MY ASSISTANTS,

JAN ROSE AND TRISH BRYANT.

WITHOUT THEIR HELP, PARTICULARLY THEIR ATTENTION TO DETAIL,

THIS BOOK AND NONE OF THE OTHER PROJECTS I'VE DONE OVER THE YEARS

WOULD HAVE BEEN POSSIBLE. THANK YOU!

CONTENTS

Flowers

ACKNOWLEDGMENTS

The book you are holding in your hands was made possible with a lot of help from many folks I'd like to thank. Information was gathered from every national park in the United States and Canada included in this book. I received nothing but friendly help when I called each park for some bit of information to include in the book. In particular, I'd like to thank Janice Smith and Leta Elford from Waterton Park and Dr. John Woods and Tamara Lamb from Revelstoke Park. Tara Luna from East Glacier Park was very helpful, meeting me a few times and hiking into the backcountry in Glacier looking for plants in bloom—where we found everything I was seeking. Diane and Mike McIvor from Banff suggested numerous locations for me to check out. Gareth Thomson from Canmore also gave me ideas and suggested places to check out. And thank you to Jim Pena for getting up in the middle of the night and joining me on a one-day trip to Glacier because I had heard that *Viola canadensis* was in bloom and I needed to photograph it—and we found it.

Pasque flower
(Pulsatilla occidentalis)

Jan and Allen Rose looked for flowers all summer for me on their property in the woods and called me every time something was in bloom; if they weren't home when I showed up, Jan would put orange flags on trees and brush to lead me to a plant in flower—how easy it was. And thanks to Jan and Allen for greeting me with smiles and great attitudes when I'd show up at their house at 5 A.M. to catch the good light. Thanks to Linda Langness for reading and editing the manuscript and making suggestions to improve the written part of the book. Doug Henderson from the University of Idaho Herbarium corrected many errors that I made in my plant descriptions. His help was invaluable. Doug taught me a great deal about how to write a plant description that both made sense and could actually be used by an observer. The librarians at the Boundary County Library in Idaho were always kind and helpful every time I walked through the door with a new list of obscure books that I needed to get through the inter-library loan system. They found them all!

I'd like to thank the following people at Fulcrum Publishing for cleaning up the manuscript, keeping me calm, and making the overall book more usable and understandable: Dan Forrest-Bank, Marlene Blessing, Ellen Wheat, and Michele Wynn.

And thanks to my partner, Vicki Long, for going on trip after trip and hike after hike into the mountains with me and finding numerous beautiful blooms for me to photograph. Again, without all of your help this book wouldn't have been possible.

INTRODUCTION

This guidebook presents ninety-five selected species of wildflowers common to the Rocky Mountain region of the United States and Canada, integrating quoted comments from adventurers who wrote about them. The flowers I have selected for inclusion are those that a visitor to the area will be most likely to find. Although not all the flowers described and illustrated here grow throughout the Rocky Mountains, a majority of them can be found in most parts of the region.

This book also reflects the views of explorers, naturalists, and early visitors who ventured into the Rockies and encountered these wildflowers in their travels. For

Yellow lady's slipper
(Cypripedium calceolus)

example, the selected quotes range from those made by such well-known naturalists as Henry David Thoreau to the journal entries of the Canadian Sir Sanford Fleming, engineer-in-chief of surveying for the trans-Canada railway project. In addition, I have included some remarks by armchair nature lovers who never actually visited the Western part of North America. Through their writings, however, they helped to nurture the love of wild places so prevalent today. Throughout, I have tried to include quoted commentary that I felt would point out something special or particularly interesting about the flower or the area where it was seen. I have been hiking, backpacking, and climbing in the Rocky Mountain ecosystem since 1973. Since 1976, I have lived in Bonners Ferry, Idaho, which is in the Selkirk Mountains, just west of the Rockies. In my explorations, I have visited many of the places that are talked about in this book.

Many of the people who live in or visit the Rocky Mountain region spend time in one or more of the major national parks that straddle the spine of this spectacular mountain chain. The section that follows includes maps of each of the parks in the United States and Canada, pinpointing the locations where explorers saw particular flowers during their travels—in Banff, Glacier, Jasper, Kootenay-Yoho, Rocky Mountain, Waterton-Glacier, and Yellowstone National Parks. Please note that these are not the only locations in the Rockies where those flowers grow.

This book covers the Rocky Mountain region from Colorado's Rocky Mountain National Park in the United States, north through Jasper National Park in Alberta, Canada. Its use eastward becomes limited once the Great Plains are reached. The flora does not change as quickly when moving westward, so this guide can be used throughout much of British Columbia, western Montana, most of Idaho (except for the desert areas in the southern portion), and parts of eastern Washington.

You will notice when using this guide that many of these wildflowers have numerous common names. The same plant may possess a different common name in other parts of the United States, as well as in Canada or elsewhere in the world. In the mid-eighteenth century, the Swedish botanist Carolus Linnaeus developed the binomial system for naming plants and animals. Each plant and animal was given one Latin name, often derived from Greek, which consisted of two words. The first word—the genus name—is always capitalized. The same genus name is assigned to plants or animals having similar characteristics. To identify a specific plant or animal, a second word—the specific epithet—is added to the genus name. The specific epithet is not capitalized and sometimes, but not always, tells us something specific about the plant or animal. For example, the specific epithet of spring beauty is *lanceolata*, which means "lance-shaped" and refers to the shape of the plant's two leaves. The genus name and specific epithet together form a species name that is internationally recognized for each plant and animal on our planet. Using this binomial system instead of employing only common names eliminates confusion because each plant and animal thus has only one valid name.

For ease of identification, I have followed tradition and have organized this book by flower color, with major sections for white and greenish-white; yellow; pink and red; blue and violet; and brown. Within those sections, the wildflowers are arranged in alphabetical order according to their Latin names (given in parentheses). Each of the color sections is introduced by a quoted passage containing the observations of an explorer of the Rocky Mountain region. These descriptions are intended to give the reader a general sense of the way early adventurers and naturalists responded to the grandeur of these spectacular mountains.

Each of the flower entries is headed by the common name of the plant, followed by its Latin name (genus and specific epithet) and family name. As a professional wildflower photographer and naturalist myself, I have found it very handy on trekking expeditions to keep notes on the flowers I find. I revisit many places, and by checking my notes, I know what was blooming at a certain location and time of year.

Subsections under each entry provide characteristic information for each plant. I begin by noting other names for the plant, if there are any. An explanation of the plant's name source follows, with comments on how the common name came about and factual or historical information about its binomial name. The next subsection provides standard flower descriptions, written in simple language with a minimum of botanical terms (a glossary at the end of the book explains any potentially confusing botanical terms). All measurements are given in both inches and centimeters. Following this you will find a description of the preferred habitat of the plant, although you should keep in mind that plants can often be found growing outside of their preferred habitat. Next, the approximate blooming time is noted. It is important to remember that flowering times vary with local weather conditions, exposure to the sun or shade, elevation, and precipitation.

The final subsection for each entry, "Comments," contains anything else of interest about the plant, including discussion of how Native Americans used the plant, its edibility for people and wildlife, its medicinal properties, and remarks on any other closely related plants you might find growing in the Rocky Mountain region. Here you

Mountain gentian
(Gentiana calycosa)

will find the quoted observations of explorers, naturalists, and early visitors to the region, whose comments are as varied as the weather in the Rockies in summer. Some of these observers merely listed the flowers they encountered during their travels, whereas others wrote detailed commentaries about a particular flower. Some passages stress the natural history of the area where the flower was found; others impart more about the writers themselves. These wildflower observers range in temperament from the sedate Lieutenant G. C. Doane, who penned a bland description of the thimbleberry he found growing on the shores of Yellowstone Lake in Yellowstone National Park, to the overly romantic vignette offered by Agnes Laut about forget-me-nots in Waterton-Glacier International Peace Park. But all of them can teach us something about perceptions of nature in earlier times.

In doing my research, I was usually able to unearth at least one historical comment about each flower, although there were a few flowers about which I was unable to find any interesting passage at all. At the other extreme, sometimes I came upon too many comments pertaining to a particular flower. The blue camas, for instance, attracted the notice of nearly every traveler through the region—over ten pages' worth in my project notes—which forced me to settle on those passages that seemed most interesting. Father DeSmet, a Belgian Jesuit missionary, correctly reflected the sentiment of the period when he called the blue camas "the queen root of the clime [climate]." I have also included a few quotes that do not refer to flowers but are designed to provide the reader with a window into the thoughts and feelings of the explorers as they traveled through the Rocky Mountain region. Also, after I came across mention of traditional uses of some of the plants by Native American and First Nations Peoples, I conferred with tribal members from both the United States and Canada and concluded that it was most acceptable to them to use the term "Native American" in the text to refer to tribes from both countries.

At the end of the book, you will find a bibliography listing the sources for the explorers' quotations about wildflowers. There is also a thorough index to facilitate your use of this guide. It includes plants listed by their common names, their binomial names, and a list of all the explorers quoted and the flowers they described.

When you use this guide in your own explorations, I strongly suggest that you avoid eating any part of a wild plant unless you are in the field with a trained naturalist who can positively identify the plant. Some edible species of plants have deadly poisonous relatives that are similar in appearance. Do not use this book or any other book to judge a plant's edibility.

Finally, wildflowers are one of the most beautiful aspects of nature's bounty. When you are out looking for them, please refrain from picking them, which deprives the next person of seeing their beauty, kills plants that have delicate root systems, and prevents those plants from forming seeds for self-propagation. Furthermore, in the national parks of the United States and Canada, picking or digging up wildflowers is illegal. Today, some nurseries and seed companies specialize in growing native plants. By purchasing plants or seeds from a nursery, you are leaving nature's garden for the next person to enjoy.

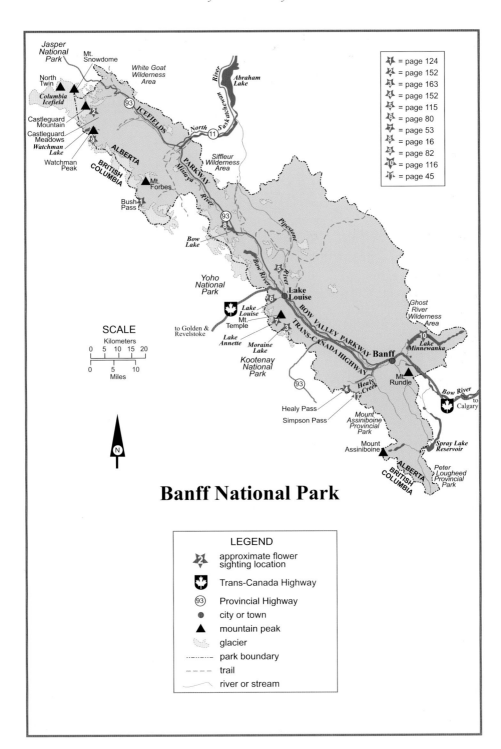

= page 124
= page 152
= page 163
= page 152
= page 115
= page 80
= page 53
= page 16
= page 82
= page 116
= page 45

SCALE

Kilometers
0 5 10 15 20

0   5   10
Miles

N

Banff National Park

LEGEND

approximate flower sighting location

Trans-Canada Highway

93 Provincial Highway

● city or town

▲ mountain peak

glacier

····· park boundary

- - - trail

river or stream

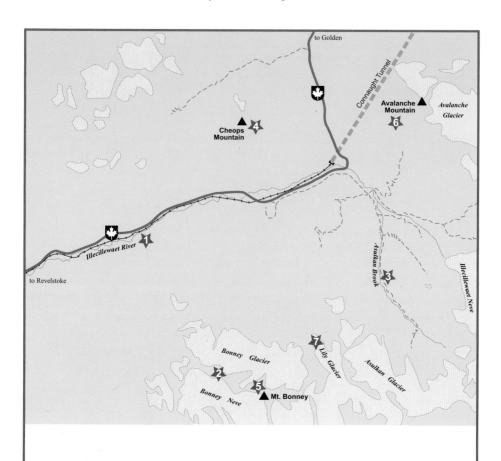

to Golden

Connaught Tunnel

Avalanche
Mountain

Avalanche
Glacier

Cheops
Mountain

Illecillewaet River

to Revelstoke

Asulkan Brook

Illecillewaet Neve

Lily Glacier

Bonney Glacier

Asulkan Glacier

Bonney Neve

▲ Mt. Bonney

Glacier National Park—Canada

SCALE

Kilometers

0   1   2

0   0.5   1

Miles

N

LEGEND

approximate flower
sighting location

Trans-Canada Highway

▲ mountain peak

glacier

·—·—·—· park boundary

– – – – trail

river or stream

+–+–+–+ railroad

Glacier
National
Park

area
shown
above

= page 97
= page 144
= page 59
= page 12
= page 42
= page 43
= page 69

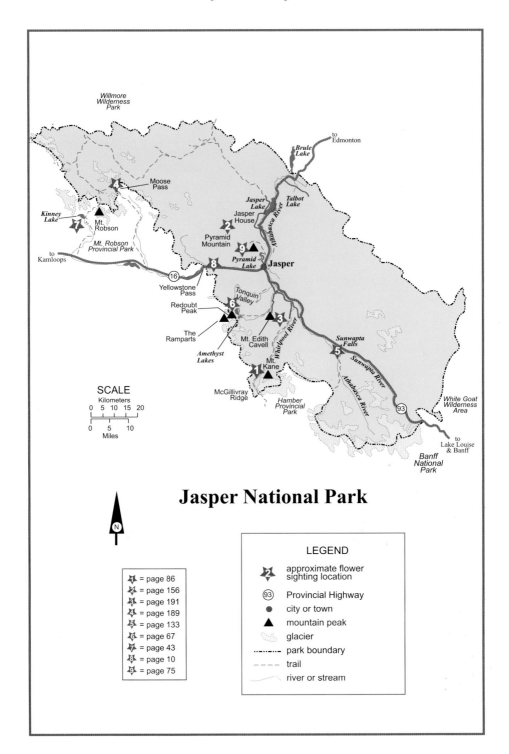

Jasper National Park

SCALE
Kilometers
0 5 10 15 20

0 5 10
Miles

Willmore
Wilderness
Park

to
Edmonton

*Brule
Lake*

Moose
Pass

*Jasper
Lake* *Talbot
Lake*

*Kinney
Lake*

Jasper
House

Mt.
Robson

*Mt. Robson
Provincial Park*

Pyramid
Mountain

to
Kamloops

*Pyramid
Lake* **Jasper**

16

Yellowstone
Pass

*Tonquin
Valley*

Redoubt
Peak

*Sunwapta
Falls*

The
Ramparts

Mt. Edith
Cavell

*Amethyst
Lakes*

Mt.
Kane

McGillivray
Ridge

*Hamber
Provincial
Park*

*White Goat
Wilderness
Area*

93

to
Lake Louise
& Banff

*Banff
National
Park*

N

LEGEND

| = page 86
| = page 156
| = page 191
| = page 189
| = page 133
| = page 67
| = page 43
| = page 10
| = page 75

approximate flower
sighting location

93 Provincial Highway

● city or town

▲ mountain peak

glacier

park boundary

trail

river or stream

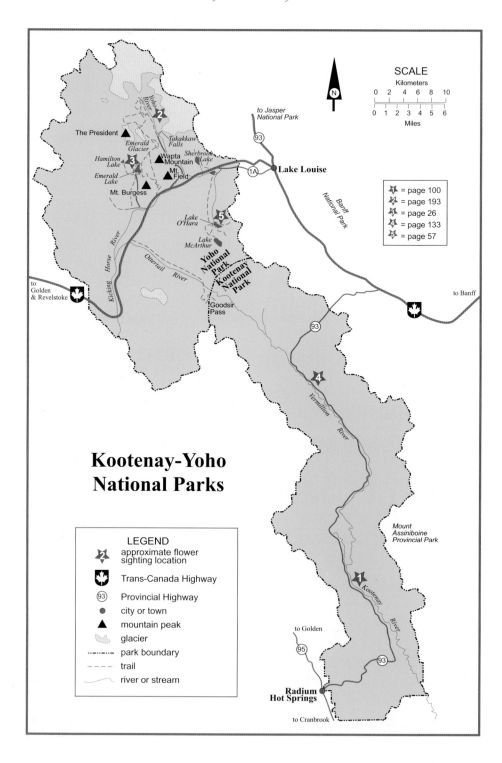

SCALE

Kilometers
0 2 4 6 8 10

0 1 2 3 4 5 6
Miles

N

to Jasper
National Park

to Golden
& Revelstoke

to Banff

to Golden

to Cranbrook

Lake Louise

The President

Emerald
Glacier

Takakkaw
Falls

Hamilton
Lake

Wapta
Mountain

Sherbrooke
Lake

Emerald
Lake

Mt.
Field

Mt. Burgess

Lake
O'Hara

Lake
McArthur

Yoho River

Yoho
National
Park

Kootenay
National
Park

Goodsir
Pass

Kicking Horse River

Ottertail River

Banff National Park

Vermillion River

Kootenay River

Mount
Assiniboine
Provincial Park

Radium
Hot Springs

= page 100
= page 193
= page 26
= page 133
= page 57

Kootenay-Yoho
National Parks

LEGEND

approximate flower
sighting location

Trans-Canada Highway

Provincial Highway

city or town

mountain peak

glacier

park boundary

trail

river or stream

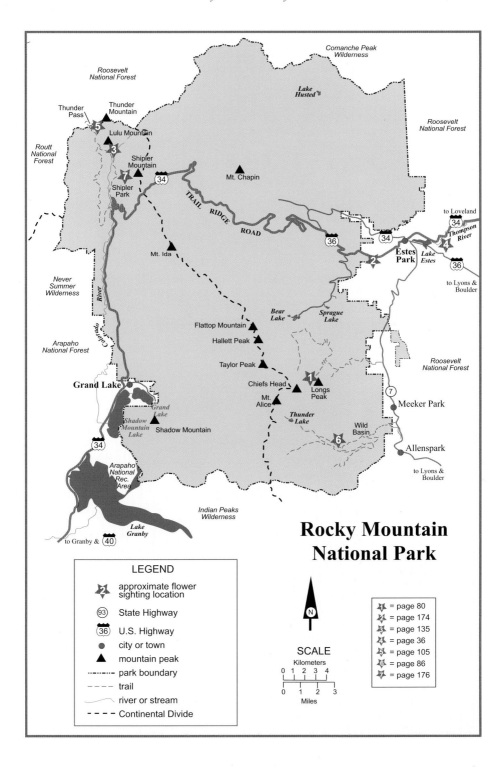

Rocky Mountain National Park

Roosevelt National Forest

Comanche Peak Wilderness

Lake Husted

Thunder Pass

Thunder Mountain

Lulu Mountain

Routt National Forest

Shipler Mountain

Shipler Park

Mt. Chapin

TRAIL RIDGE ROAD

to Loveland

Roosevelt National Forest

Thompson River

Mt. Ida

Never Summer Wilderness

Colorado River

Estes Park

Lake Estes

to Lyons & Boulder

Bear Lake

Sprague Lake

Arapaho National Forest

Flattop Mountain

Hallett Peak

Taylor Peak

Chiefs Head

Mt. Alice

Longs Peak

Roosevelt National Forest

Meeker Park

Grand Lake

Grand Lake

Shadow Mountain Lake

Shadow Mountain

Thunder Lake

Wild Basin

Allenspark

Arapaho National Rec. Area

Indian Peaks Wilderness

to Lyons & Boulder

Lake Granby

to Granby & 40

LEGEND

approximate flower sighting location

93 State Highway

36 U.S. Highway

● city or town

▲ mountain peak

·····― park boundary

― ― ― trail

river or stream

― ― ― Continental Divide

N

SCALE

Kilometers
0 1 2 3 4

0 1 2 3
Miles

= page 80
= page 174
= page 135
= page 36
= page 105
= page 86
= page 176

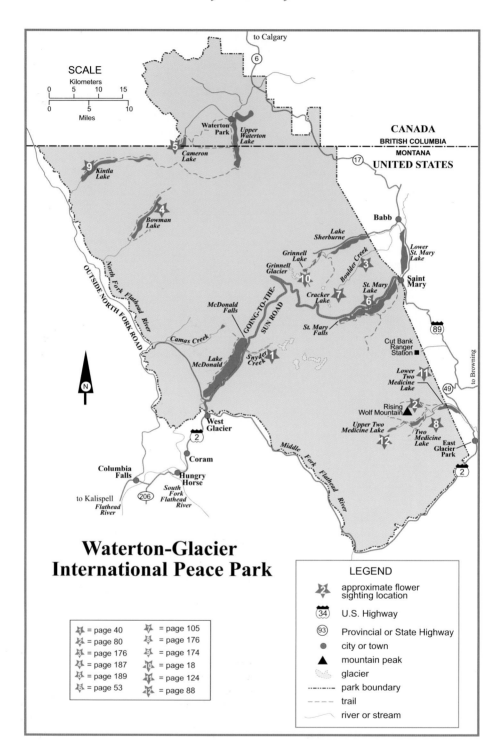

SCALE

Kilometers
0   5   10   15

0   5   10
Miles

to Calgary

6

Waterton
Park

Upper
Waterton
Lake

CANADA
BRITISH COLUMBIA
MONTANA
UNITED STATES

17

Cameron
Lake

5

9 Kintla
Lake

4 Bowman
Lake

Babb

Lake
Sherburne

Lower
St. Mary
Lake

Grinnell
Lake

Grinnell
Glacier

10

Boulder Creek

3

St. Mary
Lake

Saint
Mary

7

Cracker
Lake

6

McDonald
Falls

St. Mary
Falls

Camas Creek

Cut Bank
Ranger
Station ■

89

Lake
McDonald

Snyder
Creek

1

Lower
Two
Medicine
Lake

11

to Browning

West
Glacier

2

Rising
Wolf Mountain ▲

2

49

Middle Fork Flathead River

Upper Two
Medicine Lake

12

Two
Medicine
Lake

8

East
Glacier
Park

2

Columbia
Falls

Coram

Hungry
Horse

206

South
Fork
Flathead
River

to Kalispell
Flathead
River

OUTSIDE NORTH FORK ROAD

North Fork Flathead River

GOING-TO-THE-SUN ROAD

N

Waterton-Glacier
International Peace Park

🌼 = page 40	🌼 = page 105
🌼 = page 80	🌼 = page 176
🌼 = page 176	🌼 = page 174
🌼 = page 187	🌼 = page 18
🌼 = page 189	🌼 = page 124
🌼 = page 53	🌼 = page 88

LEGEND

🌼   approximate flower
      sighting location

(34)   U.S. Highway

(93)   Provincial or State Highway

●   city or town

▲   mountain peak

〰   glacier

····· park boundary

- - - trail

〰   river or stream

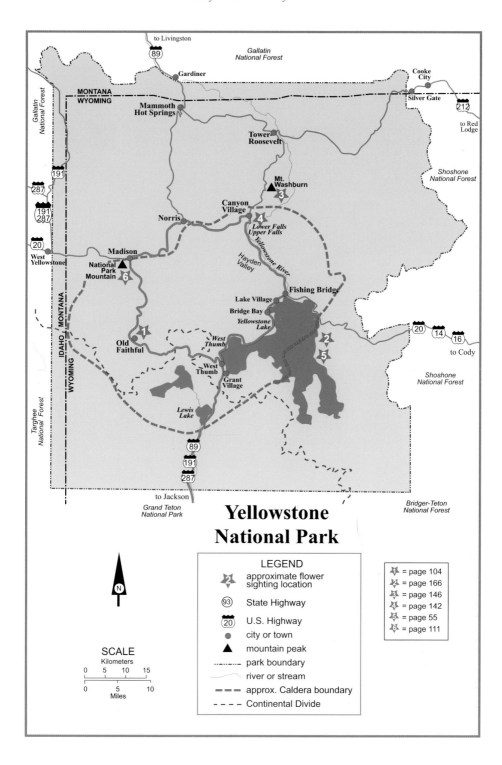

to Livingston

Gallatin
National Forest

MONTANA
WYOMING

Gallatin
National Forest

Gardiner

Cooke
City

Silver Gate

Mammoth
Hot Springs

to Red
Lodge

Shoshone
National Forest

Tower-
Roosevelt

Mt.
Washburn

3

Canyon
Village

4

Lower Falls
Upper Falls

Norris

Yellowstone River

*Hayden
Valley*

Madison

National
Park
Mountain

6

West
Yellowstone

Lake Village

Fishing Bridge

Bridge Bay

*Yellowstone
Lake*

Old
Faithful

1

*West
Thumb*

2

5

to Cody

West
Thumb

Grant
Village

Shoshone
National Forest

*Lewis
Lake*

IDAHO MONTANA

WYOMING

*Targhee
National Forest*

to Jackson

Grand Teton
National Park

Bridger-Teton
National Forest

Yellowstone
National Park

N

LEGEND

approximate flower
sighting location

93 State Highway

20 U.S. Highway

city or town

▲ mountain peak

.... park boundary

river or stream

— — — approx. Caldera boundary

- - - - Continental Divide

= page 104
= page 166
= page 146
= page 142
= page 55
= page 111

SCALE
Kilometers

0   5   10   15

0   5   10
Miles

Forget-me-not
(*Myosotis alpestris*)

FLOWERS

A meadow with beargrass *(Xerophyllum tenax)*.

White and
Greenish-White Flowers

✳

OUR REAL OBJECT WAS TO DELVE INTO THE HEART OF AN UNTOUCHED LAND, TO TREAD WHERE NO HUMAN FOOT HAD TROD BEFORE, TO TURN UNTHUMBED PAGES OF AN UNREAD BOOK, AND TO LEARN DAILY THOSE SECRETS WHICH DEAR MOTHER NATURE IS SO WILLING TO TELL TO THOSE WHO SEEK. . . . THERE IS NO VOICE . . . THAT CAN ATTUNE ITSELF TO THE LONELY CORNERS OF THE HEART, AS THE SIGH OF THE WIND THROUGH THE PINES WHEN THE TIRED EYES ARE CLOSING AFTER A DAY ON THE TRAIL. THERE IS NO CHORUS SWEETER THAN THE LITTLE BIRDS IN THE EARLY NORTHERN DAWN; AND WHAT PICTURES CAN STIR EVERY ARTISTIC NERVE MORE THAN TO GAZE FROM SOME DEEP GREEN VALLEY TO STONY CRAGS FAR ABOVE, AND SEE A BAND OF MOUNTAIN-SHEEP, IN RIGID STATUESQUE POSE.

–Nineteenth-century adventurer
Mary Schaffer, 1907

YARROW
(Achillea millefolium)

Composite Family

NAME SOURCE: The genus name, *Achillea*, is given in historical reference to the Greek warrior Achilles, said to have possibly used this plant to treat his wounded soldiers at the siege of Troy. The specific epithet, *millefolium*, means "thousand leaves" and refers to the plant's numerous leaflets, the blades of which are highly dissected and appear fernlike. The common name, yarrow, refers to the parish of Yarrow on the Yarrow River in Scotland. Its other common names, knight's milfoil, soldier's woundwort, and herb militaris, refer to the plant's medicinal properties.

DESCRIPTION: An aromatic perennial, it grows ten to forty inches (25–100 cm) tall and has many feathery fernlike leaflets on a tough stem and small white or sometimes pinkish flowers at the top in a compound inflorescence. Each inflorescence has a few small flowers, whose heads are arranged in a flat-topped cluster. The small flowers in the inflorescence are similar to the flowers of the daisy. A cluster of disk flowers in the center is surrounded by three to five ray flowers. The white ray flowers are about one-eighth inch (3 mm) long. Its aromatic, fernlike leaflets are intricately divided into fine segments. The leaflets are three to four inches (7.5–10 cm) long and up to one and one-half inches (3.8 cm) wide.

HABITAT: Yarrow grows in a variety of habitats, from dry to moderately moist soil, and from low to high alpine elevations. It does not like deep shade or wet meadows.

SEASON: April to September.

COMMENTS: Yarrow is one of the world's more common plants. It has a long history of medicinal uses. The crushed leaves will supposedly stop bleeding and alleviate toothaches. A tea made from the dried leaves is good for fevers, making the patient sweat profusely. Yarrow tea can also be used as a tonic. The Swedish botanist Linnaeus (1707–1778) claimed that beer brewed with yarrow leaves was much more intoxicating than beer brewed with hops.

BANEBERRY
(*Actaea rubra*)
Buttercup Family

NAME SOURCE: The genus name, *Actaea*, is from the Greek word *aktea*, which means "elder." This refers to its leaves, which are similar to elder leaves in shape, though not in texture. The specific epithet, *rubra*, means "red" and refers to the color of the plant's berry. "Bane," in the common name, is a word applied to plants suspected of being poisonous.

DESCRIPTION: A perennial, it grows up to three feet (90 cm) tall, with an erect branched stem that has several sharply toothed large leaves. Each stem terminates in a short raceme that is rounded on top and composed of numerous tiny white flowers. The flowers have three to five sepals that quickly fall off once the flower opens. The four or five white petals are each shaped like a spatula and are about one-eighth inch (3 mm) long. The numerous stamens give the flower raceme a fuzzy appearance. The fruit is a glistening red (or sometimes white) berry that appears in clusters. Each berry is one-fourth to one-half inch (6–13 mm) wide and contains a

The berries of baneberry contain
a few coral-red seeds.

few coral-red seeds. The leaves are very characteristic of all members of the Buttercup Family, being three-parted, lobed, or compounded, and always on a basis of three.

HABITAT: Moist woods and along streams, often in shady areas.

SEASON: May to July.

COMMENTS: All parts of this plant, especially the berry, are poisonous. Baneberry is a fairly nondescript plant until its berries appear. The berries ripen about the same time as huckleberries.

SERVICEBERRY
(*Amelanchier alnifolia*)
Rose Family

OTHER NAMES: Juneberry, shadberry, Saskatoon berry, Indian pears, sarvisberry.

NAME SOURCE: The specific epithet, *alnifolia*, refers to the similarity between its leaves and those of the alder. The common names serviceberry and sarvisberry refer to its resemblance to the English service tree (*Sorbus domestica*).

DESCRIPTION: A common shrub, it becomes three to ten feet (1–3 m) tall, with bright green leaves and clusters of white flowers. When in full bloom, the flowers entirely cover the plant. The numerous flowers are composed of five narrow white petals, usually twisted and about one-half inch (1.3 cm) long. The flowers commonly have twenty stamens. The plant's bright green leaves are oval to elliptic-oblong, with teeth on the edges toward the rounded tip. The leaves are one to two inches (2.5–5 cm) long. Its fruit is a juicy bluish-purple pome that resembles the blueberry and is about one-half inch (1.3 cm) in diameter. The sweet-tasting pome contains several seeds.

HABITAT: A variety of habitats, from stream banks to moist hillsides to open woods and from low to middle elevations.

SEASON: April to July.

COMMENTS: The fruit crop was very important to Native Americans. Various wildlife species eat the current year's plant growth. Pheasant, grouse, songbirds, black bear, and others eat the pomes. The buds are a staple winter food of the ruffed grouse. Elk, deer, moose, and other wildlife species browse the plant.

Meriwether Lewis of the Lewis and Clark Expedition wrote: "The natives sometimes eat the berries without preparation; sometimes they dry them in the sun . . . they very frequently pound and bake them in large loaves, weighing from 10 to 15 pounds. The bread keeps very well for one season, and retains its juices better by this mode of preparation than any other. When broken, it is stirred in cold water until it acquires the consistency of soup, and then eaten." The serviceberry was the main fruit used in making pemmican, the iron ration that sustained many travelers on their Western journeys.

David Thompson, a Canadian explorer and geographer who was active in the Canadian Rockies in the early 1800s, wrote: "Pemican, a wholesome, well tasted nutritious food is made of the lean parts of the bison dried, smoked, and pounded

When serviceberry is in full bloom,
the flowers cover the plant entirely.

fine . . . called Beat Meat. Pemican is made up of twenty pounds of soft and the same of hard fat, slowly melted together, and poured on fifty pounds of Beat Meat, well mixed together and closely packed. On the Great Plains there is a shrub [serviceberry] bearing a very sweet berry of a dark colour, much sought after, great quantities are dried by the Natives and . . . mixed to make Pemican."

In 1861–1863, Viscount Milton and W. B. Cheadle traveled the length of Canada, crossing the Continental Divide by way of Yellowhead Pass in July 1863, then following the Fraser River to Tete Jaune Cache. After being ferried across the Fraser River in canoes by a group of Shushwap Indians, Cheadle wrote in his diary that night: "We resolved to rest a day here, in order to thoroughly overhaul our provisions, after their recent wettings, and obtain what information we could from the Shushwaps concerning our future course. The Indians brought in a plentiful supply of the poire, wild pear, or service berry, which we purchased for some needles and thread. This fruit. . . is said by the Hudson's Bay people that wherever it flourishes wheat will also grow to perfection. The berry is about the size of a black currant, pear-shaped, and of delicious sweetness and flavour. They are much used by the Indians on both sides of the mountains" (Cheadle: No. 8 on Jasper National Park map).

PEARLY EVERLASTING
(*Anaphalis margaritacea*)
COMPOSITE FAMILY

OTHER NAMES: Life-everlasting.

NAME SOURCE: The specific epithet, *margaritacea*, means "pearly" in Latin, describing the flowers. The common name, everlasting, refers to the dried flower heads' appearing essentially the same as fresh ones, thus they last forever.

DESCRIPTION: An erect perennial, eight to thirty-six inches (20–90 cm) tall, it displays unbranched clustered stems with numerous narrow leaves topped by small buttonlike flower heads. The entire plant is densely white-woolly. The flower heads are about one-fourth inch (6 mm) long and made up of mostly pearly white bracts that surround the very tiny pale yellow flowers in the center of the head. The numerous narrow, lance-shaped leaves, two to five inches (5–12.5 cm) long, are evenly distributed along the woolly stem. The undersides of the leaves are much woollier than the upper sides.

HABITAT: Open places and along roadsides.

SEASON: June to September.

COMMENTS: Frederick King Butters wrote about the flora of Glacier National Park in Canada for the 1932 *Canadian Alpine Journal*: "One of the most characteristic features of the Selkirk Range is the extraordinarily dense vegetation which chokes the narrow valleys and clothes the lower slopes of the mountains." This is still true of most of this park's forested areas. Butters also noted "a few burned-over tracts near Glacier, especially on the south slopes of Mt. Cheops. . . . In such places there is usually a great abundance of fireweed, everlasting [pearly everlasting], white-

Pearly everlasting has buttonlike flower heads.

flowered hawkweed and bracken. . . . If left to themselves these clearings tend to revert to forest, but the change is necessarily slow and for decades they retain their peculiar character" (Butters: No. 4 on Glacier National Park map).

RED-STEMMED CEANOTHUS
(Ceanothus sanguineus)
BUCKTHORN FAMILY

OTHER NAMES: Buckbrush, snowbrush.

NAME SOURCE: The specific epithet, *sanguineus*, refers to the blood-red stems. This shrub is a favorite browse of deer, thus its common name, buckbrush. The other common name, snowbrush, came about because from a distance this shrub appears to be covered with freshly fallen snow when it is in full bloom.

DESCRIPTION: A large shrub, three to almost ten feet (1–3 m) tall, it has oval leaves, smooth reddish branches, and numerous tiny cream-white flowers growing in crowded branching clusters. Each flower in the numerous clusters has five sepals, five petals, and five stamens. The flower is very distinctive because of its hooded petals. The oval to heart-shaped alternate leaves are about two inches (5 cm) long and have a distinct leafstalk. There are three main veins radiating from near the base of the leaf blade.

HABITAT: Moist soil of hills and mountain slopes and in burned-over areas.

SEASON: June to July.

COMMENTS: In winter and early spring, it is a major part of the deer diet. Elk and rabbit also browse this shrub. It often grows in dense patches. When you take some of the flowers and rub them between your palms, a soapy froth develops.

Red-stemmed ceanothus is also known as snowbrush because in full bloom it appears to be covered with freshly fallen snow.

SPRING BEAUTY
(Claytonia lanceolata)
PURSLANE FAMILY

OTHER NAMES: Groundnut, good morning spring.

NAME SOURCE: The genus name, *Claytonia*, honors the American botanist John Clayton (1686–1773), who did much of his plant collecting in Virginia. The specific epithet, lanceolata, means "lance-shaped" and describes the plant's two leaves on each stem.

DESCRIPTION: A small perennial with a few to several delicate stems, it grows two to eight inches (5–20 cm) tall. Each stem has a pair of lance-shaped succulent leaves and white or pink bowl-shaped small flowers in a raceme above the leaves. The dainty flowers of the loose terminal raceme have five white to pinkish petal-like sepals that are pink-lined, notched at the tip, and from one-fourth to one inch (6–25 mm) wide. The flower has five stamens. The pair of narrow lance-shaped leaves occurs at about mid-stem. They are opposite, stalkless, and one to four inches (2.5–10 cm) long. The plant grows from a deeply buried corm.

HABITAT: Moist ground near snowbanks, from low to alpine elevations.

SEASON: April to July, depending on the elevation.

COMMENTS: The raw corm has a radishlike taste and when boiled has the texture and taste of potatoes. Spring beauty is one of the first white or pink flowers to appear in spring, often forming dense populations and frequently found blooming at the edge of snowbanks. Elk, deer, and mountain sheep graze it in the spring. Grizzly bear, squirrel, marmot, and pocket gopher eat its corms.

In 1872 and 1873, John Coulter served as assistant geologist to the U.S. Geological Geographical Survey of the Territories headed by Ferdinand Vandeveer Hayden, after whom Hayden Valley in Yellowstone Park is named. Coulter later became a prominent U.S. botanist. The 1872 survey team worked in the Tetons and Yellowstone, moving on to Colorado in 1873. Coulter collected and dried plants from every area where he worked. He and several others climbed the 14,286-foot Mt. Lincoln, about fifty miles south of Rocky Mountain National Park. His journal noted: "The ascent as made on July 9th, 1873, a highly favorable time to see mountain plants in all their glory. . . . Early we commenced the climb and every step in advance brought us to new beauties, and long before the summit was reached our portfolios were groaning with treasures which neither love nor money nor fatigue could have induced us to throw away." At the summit, he wrote, "We could see to the north Long [Longs Peak] and Gray and Torrey and a host of their equals, and far to the south rose that great isolated mountain of Pike's Peak. . . . I cannot leave Mt. Lincoln without saying a word about the lovely Alpine flowers . . . growing on its heights, and in fact on all the mountains here, covering with beauty the grassy slopes on the rocky declivities from timber-line to the very summit. Conspicuous . . . are the Claytonias, or 'Spring Beauties,' with their delicate penciled petals; the exquisite deep blue of the 'Forget-me-not'; Phloxes of every shade of white and purple and blue, and hosts of others."

Mary Schaffer recounted her explorations of the Canadian Rockies in 1907–1908 in Old Indian Trails. Of Bow Lake in Banff National Park she commented, "Never have I seen the lake look more beautiful than on that fair morning in June. It was as blue as the sky could make it, the ice reflected the most vivid emerald green; in the distance a fine glacier swept to the lake-shore, whose every crevasse was a brilliant blue line; the bleak grey mountains towered above, at our feet the bright spring flowers bloomed in the green grass, and over all hung the deep blue sky. Around us hovered the peace which only the beauty and silence of the hills could portray. . . . Winter was reluctantly loosening its hard grasp upon those open meadow-like slopes; the snow lilies, the pale pink spring beauties, and the bright yellow violets were flirting with the butterflies and bees, pretending to be utterly oblivious to the mountains of snow all about them" (Schaffer: No. 8 on Banff National Park map).

BEADLILY
(*Clintonia uniflora*)

LILY FAMILY

OTHER NAMES: Queen's cup, bride's bonnet, queen's cup beadlily.

NAME SOURCE: The genus name, *Clintonia*, honors New York state's Governor DeWitt Clinton (1769–1828), a botanist and naturalist of much ability. The specific epithet, uniflora, means "one-flowered." The common name, beadlily, refers to the plant's deep blue fruits, which look like polished lapis lazuli.

DESCRIPTION: This creeping perennial has one pure white, fairly large flower that blooms on a short, leafless stalk, up to six inches (15 cm) tall, amid a cluster of two to three upright shiny elliptic leaves. The bell-shaped flower is composed of six similar lance-shaped petal-like segments and is one to one and one-half inches (2.5–3.8 cm) wide. The flower has six yellow stamens. The creeping rootstalk gives rise to pairs of upright slenderly elliptic leaves, each with a flowering stem in their midst. The leaves have fine short hairs along their margins and undersurface and are two and one-half to six inches (6.3–15 cm) long and two to three inches (5–7.5 cm) wide. The leaves are generally longer than the flowering stems. The fruit is a solitary, deep blue, inedible berry borne erect on the fruiting stem after the flowering.

HABITAT: Damp coniferous forests.

SEASON: May to June.

COMMENTS: The ruffed grouse eats the blue berry, not considered palatable by humans. It often grows in the same area with bunchberry dogwood (*Cornus canadensis*).

In *Your National Parks* (1917), Enos Mills provided a thorough description of U.S. and Canadian national parks of the time. He praised Waterton-Glacier Park for its "scores of varieties of flowers. These brighten the woods, stand along the streams, border the lakes, and crowd close to other glaciers. They climb above the limits of tree growth. Grinnell Lake has a grand wild-flower garden on its shores. Among the many kinds are bluebell, queen's-cup [beadlily], violet, water-lily, and wild hollyhock" (Mills: No. 10 on Waterton-Glacier International Peace Park map).

BUNCHBERRY DOGWOOD
(*Cornus canadensis*)
DOGWOOD FAMILY

OTHER NAMES: Bunchberry, dwarf dogwood, plant of gluttony, dwarf cornel.

NAME SOURCE: The predominant common name, bunchberry, refers to the plant's dense cluster of bright red berries. Plant of gluttony, another common name, comes from Scotland, where people thought eating its berries would increase the appetite.

DESCRIPTION: A perennial plant, three to eight inches (7.5–20 cm) tall, it can form dense mats. Each upright stem has a whorl of elliptic leaves just below a cluster of small greenish to whitish flowers. Greenish when young, the flowers become whitish with age. The numerous tiny flowers are crowded into a tight cluster and surrounded by four large distinctive white petal-like bracts that are modified leaves. Each oval-shaped bract is about three-fourths inch (2 cm) long. Four to seven attractive elliptic leaves comprise the whorl on the upper part of each stem, ranging up to three inches (7.5 cm) long. In the fall the leaves change color before dropping to the ground.

HABITAT: Moist woods.

SEASON: May to August.

COMMENTS: The bunchberry dogwood is one of the smallest members of the genus *Cornus*. It resembles a miniature dogwood tree. Grouse eat the leaves in summer and the berries in autumn. In the moist woodland garden, the bunchberry dogwood makes an excellent groundcover.

In this passage, the indomitable Helen Keller related part of her learning experience: "We read and studied out of doors, preferring the sunlit woods to the house. All my early lessons have in them the breath of the woods, the fine, resinous odour of pine needles blended with the perfume of wild grapes. Seated in the gracious shade of a wild tulip tree, I learned to think that everything has a lesson and a suggestion. . . . Indeed, everything that could hum, or buzz, or sing, or bloom, had a part in my education—noisy-throated frogs; katydids and crickets held in my hand until, forgetting their embarrassment, they trilled their reedy note; little downy chickens and wild flowers; the dogwood blossoms; meadow-violets and budding fruit trees."

RED-OSIER DOGWOOD
(Cornus stolonifera)
DOGWOOD FAMILY

COMMON NAME: Red-osier.

NAME SOURCE: The specific epithet, *stolonifera*, refers to the plant's stolons or rooting runners. The common name, red-osier, calls attention to the red-colored branches.

DESCRIPTION: This tall shrub, growing up to thirteen feet (4 m) tall, flaunts distinctive reddish branches that have opposite oval-elliptic leaves and flat-topped clusters of small greenish-white flowers. The flowers have four oval-shaped pointed petals about one-fourth inch (6 mm) wide. The opposite oval-elliptic leaves have a short leafstalk and are one to three inches (2.5–7.5 cm) long. They are heavily veined and a lighter color on the underside. In fall, the leaves turn reddish, and white to bluish berries adorn the shrub. These berries are about one-fourth inch (6 mm) in diameter and contain one seed. In winter when the leaves have fallen from the shrub, its flexible reddish stems are very conspicuous.

This tall shrub can grow
up to twelve feet.

HABITAT: Meadows, boggy areas, and stream banks, to high in the mountains.

SEASON: May to July.

COMMENTS: Found throughout temperate North America, red-osier is very popular with many wildlife species. Rabbit, deer, elk, and moose browse the twigs and winter buds. Numerous bird species, especially the ruffed grouse and evening grosbeak, eagerly eat the berries. Native Americans roasted the white inner bark of the branches over a fire until dry, mixed it with tobacco and kinnikinnick, and smoked it. They used the flexible red-osier branch for bows and combined its sour berries with sweet serviceberries in a dessert called "Sweet and Sour."

MOUNTAIN LADY'S SLIPPER
(*Cypripedium montanum*)
ORCHID FAMILY

OTHER NAMES: Moccasin flower, white lady's slipper.

NAME SOURCE: The genus name, *Cypripedium*, literally meaning "Venus's slipper" comes from two Latin nouns: *Cypria*, a name for Venus, the goddess of love, and *pedilon*, meaning slipper. The specific epithet, *montanum*, is Latin for "of the mountains" and refers to the plant's usual habitat.

DESCRIPTION: A perennial with an erect leafy stem, eight to twenty-eight inches (20–70 cm) tall, it usually displays a solitary white to dull purple pouchlike flower at the top of the stem. The flower is composed of three purplish-brown sepals, one and one-fourth to three inches (3.1–7.5 cm) long, which are lance-shaped and twisted. It also has three petals, two of which are similar to the sepals only smaller, with the third petal forming the pouch or lip. This pouch is delicately veined with purple and from three-fourths to one and one-fourth inch (2–3.1 cm) long. Scattered along the stem are four to seven ovate to broadly lance-shaped leaves, two to six inches (5–15 cm) long. Members of the genus *Cypripedium* have two fertile stamens instead of the one or three that are common in most other members of the Orchid Family.

HABITAT: A variety of habitats from dry or moist open woods to mountain slopes.

SEASON: May to August.

COMMENTS: The flowers are very sweet-scented. *Cypripedium calceolus* is very similar to the mountain lady's slipper except that it has yellow flowers.

Lady's slippers are very different from most other members of the Orchid Family. Charles Darwin surmised that an

Yellow lady's slipper
(Cypripedium calceolus)

enormous wave of extinction eliminated many intermediate forms of orchids and left the lady's slipper as the record of the former simpler state of orchids.

On June 6, 1806, Meriwether Lewis and William Clark were camped among the Nez Perce Indians along the Clearwater River in Idaho, before they crossed the Continental Divide during their trip back east. In his journal, Lewis wrote, "Among the plants was a kind of lady's slipper or moccasin-flower, resembling that common in the United States, but with a white corolla, marked with longitudinal veins of a pale color on the inner side."

The American naturalist John Burroughs wrote about an eastern variety of lady's slipper in his book *Riverby*: "Report came to me that in a certain quaking bog in the woods the showy lady's slipper could be found. The locality proved to be the marrowy grave of an extinct lake or black tarn. The lady's slipper grew in little groups and companies all about. Never have I beheld a prettier sight, so gay, so festive, so holiday looking. Were they so many gay bonnets rising above the foliage? or were they flocks of white doves with purple-stained breasts just lifting up their wings to take flight? or were they little fleets of fairy boats with sail set, tossing on a mimic sea of wild, weedy growths? Such images throng the mind on recalling the scene and only hint at its beauty and animation."

WHITE MOUNTAIN AVENS
(*Dryas octopetala*)
ROSE FAMILY

OTHER NAMES: Mountain avens.

NAME SOURCE: The genus name, *Dryas*, is Greek for "wood nymph." For this wood nymph, the oak was sacred. The specific epithet, *octopetala*, means "eight petals," a reference to the eight-petaled flowers. A flower with eight petals is rather unusual.

DESCRIPTION: A creeping plant with oval-toothed evergreen leaves, it often grows in large patches. An erect leafless flower stalk, two to ten inches (5–25 cm) tall, supports creamy white eight-petaled flowers. The dark green, leathery, evergreen leaves, up to one and one-fourth inches (3.1 cm) long, are deeply veined and have toothed edges. The undersides of the oak-like leaves are often very hairy and white. The seed heads resemble feathery plumes.

HABITAT: Rocky, gravelly places, from middle elevations to above timberline.

SEASON: June to August.

COMMENTS: Members of the genus *Dryas* are intolerant of shade. The low growth of white mountain avens, one of the largest mat-forming plants of the alpine zone, may help protect it from the region's harsh winds and snows. It makes an excellent rock garden plant.

James Outram, in his book *In the Heart of the Canadian Rockies*, described the scenery on his hike from Emerald Lake to a climber's camp in the Yoho Valley in Yoho National Park in the early 1900s: "A magnificent view of the Takakkaw Fall

A showy blossom of white mountain avens

here challenges attention: our elevation is almost exactly that of the top of the upper fall, and the glacier-tongue, the rushing torrent from its icy cavern and the gigantic fall of seething water form a complete picture of remarkable interest and effectiveness. Part of our way lay over alps, clothed, as usual, with luxuriant flowers, the yellow mountain lily very prominent, purple asters, white dryas, and anemones also abundant" (Outram: No. 3 on Kootenay-Yoho National Park map).

In 1938, Robert Marshall, a founder of the Wilderness Society, climbed North Doonerak in the Brooks Range in northern Alaska. He described their descent from the chilly summit in his book *Alaska Wilderness*: "[W]e ran down the slide-rock to get warm. We reached a lake-filled benchland extending for miles in every direction. The sun, which had been obscured by clouds much of the afternoon, at last came out to stay and turned the mosses and leafy plants into a carpet of vivid green. Set in this carpet, everywhere as far as the eye could see, was the golden gleam of the arctic poppy and the snow white petal of the Dryas. The green, the gold, the white, all were so unblemished under the bright sunshine, the rich vegetation so entirely untouched by man, and everything around so peaceful and pure that it seemed a pattern for the Eden of men's dreams."

WILD STRAWBERRY
(*Fragaria*)
ROSE FAMILY

There are several species of *Fragaria* from the Rocky Mountain area, all of which are similar in appearance. The description below is a general one for the genus *Fragaria*.

NAME SOURCE: The genus name, *Fragaria*, is from the Latin word *frago* and means "to emit a sweet odor or fragrance." The common name, strawberry, is a descendant of the old Anglo-Saxon word "streawberige," which refers to how the plant strews its runners over the ground.

DESCRIPTION: These are low-growing perennial plants that spread by means of runners. Members of this genus have blades that are divided into three smaller leaflets. The white flowers have five petals and many yellow stamens. The flower is followed by the delicious and distinctive red fruit.

HABITAT: Shaded banks along streams and in open meadows, growing from low elevations to timberline.

SEASON: April to August.

COMMENTS: The fruit of the wild strawberry is eaten by many birds, small rodents, bear, and other wildlife species.

The British writer Izaak Walton (1593–1683) once said, "Doubtless God could have made a better berry than the Strawberry, but doubtless God never did."

Even men working in the Rocky Mountains in the 1800s succumbed to the charms of the wild strawberry. Charles Wilson was a member of the British survey team responsible for locating the 49th Parallel that was to be the boundary between Canada and the United States. Wilson's journal entry on June 3, 1860: "I rode out . . . to the plains about 8 miles from the Fort, to pay a visit to Mr. Covington who has a farm there. The plain was literally red with wild strawberries, much larger than our English ones. We laid down and in a very short time picked a large kettle full and then adjourned to the farm where we had a tremendous feast of strawberries and cream."

RATTLESNAKE PLANTAIN
(*Goodyera oblongifolia*)
ORCHID FAMILY

NAME SOURCE: The genus name, *Goodyera*, honors the English botanist John Goodyer (1592–1664). The specific epithet, *oblongifolia*, refers to the plant's oblong leaves. The common name, rattlesnake plantain, points to the plant's evergreen leaves, marked with silvery tracings that resemble the patterns on snakes.

DESCRIPTION: This plant has a rosette of dark green, white-striped, basal leaves, from which grows the erect stout stem, ten to eighteen inches (25–45 cm) tall, topped by a spike of greenish-white flowers that spiral around the stem. Its flowering spike is composed of a few to many small flowers. The petals of the flowers converge with one of the sepals to form a hood over the saclike lip. The dark green oblong-elliptic shaped leaves, which often have a white strip down the center, are up to three and one-half inches (9 cm) long.

HABITAT: Deep mossy woods.

SEASON: June to August.

COMMENTS: Henry David Thoreau wrote the following about this plant: "The leaf of the rattlesnake plantain now surprises the walker amid the dry leaves on cool hillsides in the woods; of very simple form, but richly veined with longitudinal and transverse white veins. It looks like art."

The leaves of rattlesnake plantain have a distinct white stripe down the center.

COW PARSNIP
(*Heracleum sphondylium* ssp. *montanum*)
PARSLEY FAMILY

OTHER NAMES: Cow cabbage, Hercules parsnip.

NAME SOURCE: The genus *Heracleum* is named for the Greek hero Hercules, who supposedly used parts of the plant for its medicinal properties.

DESCRIPTION: A woolly haired perennial, up to ten feet (3 m) tall, it has a hollow, many-branched stout stem that has huge leaves and is topped by small white or slightly greenish flowers in large, dense, flat-topped clusters. The tiny flowers are borne in flat-topped umbels that are from six to twelve inches (15–30 cm) wide. The numerous five-petaled flowers are about one-fourth inch (6 mm) long, with the largest flowers on the edge of the umbels. Its woolly haired leaves are six to twelve inches (15–30 cm) long and up to one foot (30 cm) wide. Long leafstalks clasp the stout stems. The blades are round and are divided into three separate leaflets that have coarsely toothed margins.

HABITAT: On stream banks and in rich damp soil.

SEASON: May to August.

COMMENTS: *Do not eat* any member of the Parsley Family until identification is absolutely positive as there are several members of this family that are deadly poisonous and look similar to the nonpoisonous species.

The leaves of cow parsnip can grow up to twelve inches long and twelve inches wide.

Elk and bear eagerly eat this plant. Worldwide, there are about sixty species of *Heracleum*. The cow parsnip is the only member of this genus native to North America.

During their Western exploration, Lewis and Clark ate many native plants, learning about the edibility of those plants from Native Americans. On May 2, 1806, near present-day Walla Walla, Washington, Lewis wrote in his journal, "The three young Wollawollahs continued with us. During the day we observed them eating the inner part of the young succulent stem of a plant. . . . On tasting this plant we found it agreeable, and ate heartily of it without any inconvenience." The plant was the cow parsnip.

OCEANSPRAY
(*Holodiscus discolor*)
ROSE FAMILY

OTHER NAMES: Cream bush, ironwood.

NAME SOURCE: The specific epithet, *discolor*, means "of two usually distinct colors" and refers to the flowers.

DESCRIPTION: An erect, many-branched shrub, it grows from three to nine feet (1–2.8 m) tall. It has dull green oval-toothed leaves and numerous tiny saucer-shaped cream-white flowers growing in dense branching clusters. The tiny flowers, about one-eighth inch (3 mm) in diameter, grow in dense hanging clusters that are two to eight inches (5–20 cm) long. Each flower has five white petals and five smaller sepals, both

**Oceanspray can grow
up to nine feet tall.**

oval-shaped. There are usually twenty stamens, arranged with three opposite each petal and one opposite each sepal. The alternate, ovate-toothed leaves, three-fourths inch to three inches (2–7.5 cm) long, are dark green above and almost white on the underside. In the fall, the leaves turn reddish.

HABITAT: Moist woods and along stream banks.

SEASON: May to August.

COMMENTS: Some Native American tribes used the ironwood for cooking utensils because of its toughness and resistance to burning quickly. The older branches are extremely hard.

OXEYE DAISY
(Leucanthemum Vulgare)
COMPOSITE FAMILY

OTHER NAMES: Moon daisy.

NAME SOURCE: The genus name, *Leucanthemum*, is from the Greek words *leukos*, meaning "white," and *anthemon*, meaning "flower." This refers to the white ray flowers.

DESCRIPTION: A leafy perennial, it becomes eight to thirty-two inches (20–80 cm) tall, with several erect clustered stems, each bearing a large solitary head of white rays surrounding a yellow center. The oxeye daisy is an excellent example of a typical Composite Family flower head. It has tiny yellow disk flowers encircled by larger white ray flowers, each resembling a single petal. The entire flower head is about 3 inches (7.5 cm) wide. Its dark green, broad, lance-shaped basal leaves, one and one-half to six inches (3.8–15 cm) long, have long leafstalks. The leaves on the upper stem are smaller, lack a leafstalk, and clasp the stem. All the leaves are coarsely toothed.

HABITAT: Pastures, fields, and along roadsides.

SEASON: May to August.

COMMENTS: There are many superstitions about the daisy. One belief is that spring has not arrived until you can step on twelve daisies at once. And supposedly, if you eat the roots of daisies, your growth will be stunted, but if you eat three flower heads of a daisy after having a tooth pulled, you'll never have a toothache again.

Luther Burbank, an American horticulturist, produced a number of new plant varieties. One of them was the popular shasta daisy, in the creation of which he used four other daisies, including the oxeye daisy.

Oxeye grows in pastures, fields, and roadsides.

It was largely through the efforts of Enos Mills that Rocky Mountain National Park was established in 1915. In several of his books, he recounted his love of nature and the beauty of the area that became Rocky Mountain National Park. He wrote, "In these mountains there are many deep gorges and canons. Most of these are short and ice-polished. The Thompson Canon is one of the longest and finest. Its twenty miles of walled length is full of scenic contrasts and picturesque varieties. . . . In places its walls stand two thousand feet above the river and the daisies. The walls are many-formed, rugged, polished, perpendicular, terraced and statuesque. . . . Blossoms fill many niches with poetry, while shrubbery, concealing in its clinging the cracks in the wall, forms many a charming festoon" (Mills: No. 4 on Rocky Mountain National Park map).

WOODNYMPH
(Moneses uniflora)

WINTERGREEN FAMILY

OTHER NAMES: One-flowered wintergreen, single delight.

NAME SOURCE: The genus name, *Moneses*, is from the Greek words *monos*, meaning "single," and *esis*, meaning "to send forth," a reference to the plant's solitary flower. The specific epithet, *uniflora*, means "one-flowered." Both the genus name and specific epithet emphasize the plant's solitary flower.

DESCRIPTION: A low evergreen plant, it grows up to five inches (12.5 cm) tall, with pear-shaped basal leaves and an unbranched flowering stem topped by a solitary, white to pinkish, waxy, nodding flower. The solitary flower is five-eighths to one inch (1.5–2.5 cm) wide and has five sepals and five triangular waxy petals ranging in color from white to pinkish-purple. The flower has ten stamens that occur in pairs and a distinctive pistil that is longer than the stamens. The basal, pear-shaped leathery leaves are finely toothed and are one inch (2.5 cm) or less in length.

HABITAT: In the moister parts of coniferous forests, often in soil that has rotting wood mixed in with it.

SEASON: Early summer.

COMMENTS: Walter Wilcox enjoyed hiking, camping, and climbing in the Canadian Rockies. In this passage from his book *The Rockies of Canada*, he described horse travel in the mountains: "The monotony of riding an Indian pony during the slow march of five or six hours as the poor beast struggles over logs and through swampy places, fighting bull-dog flies and grey gnats, is broken by that endless variety and change of surroundings, that are a source of delight in every part of these mountains. Sometimes the trail leads for a time through deep forests where the mountains are lost to view. In the cool depths of forest shade the rhododendron grows, and the moist and mossy ground is often dotted with the wax-like blossoms of the one-flowered pyrola (*Moneses*), or the pretty violet-like butterwort.

Woodnymph is a low-growing evergreen plant
with a solitary flower.

INDIAN PIPE
(Monotropa uniflora)
WINTERGREEN FAMILY

OTHER NAMES: Ghost plant.

NAME SOURCE: The genus name, *Monotropa*, is from the Greek words *mono* and *tropos*, which together mean "one direction." This refers to the plant's solitary flower, which hangs downward. The specific epithet, *uniflora*, means "one-flowered."

DESCRIPTION: A very distinctive perennial plant, four to twelve inches (10–30 cm) tall, with a downward-hanging waxy, white, bell-shaped flower attached to a waxy white stem. Usually several stems grow in a cluster. The solitary flower has five (sometimes four or six) petals that are about one inch (2.5 cm) long, and usually having ten stamens. When the plant matures, the bell-shaped flower turns upward, eventually turning black with age. The stem is almost translucent, with leaves represented by small white scales pressed against the stem. There is no green coloring whatsoever in this plant.

HABITAT: Deep shady woods.

SEASON: June to August.

COMMENTS: Indian pipe has no chlorophyll and thus can't produce its own food.
It obtains its food through a relationship
with a fungus in the soil. The fungus
obtains its nourishment from the roots of
other green plants, and the Indian pipe
then receives its food from the fungus.

Margaret Thompson, who explored
what was then Waterton Lakes National
Park in the 1930s, wrote the delightful
High Trails of Glacier National Park, an excellent guidebook giving the reader her view
of the intimate beauties of the park. After
hiking up the Snyder Creek drainage and

When indian pipe matures, the bell-shaped flower
turns upward and eventually black.

exploring the Sperry Glacier, which she described as "an event of a lifetime," she
continued: "Returning from the glacier, we have luncheon at the chalets and start
down the trail. It is seven miles to Lake McDonald. The trail winds through glacial
meadows where the yellow warbler, the goldfinch, and many other birds fill the air
with their songs, and where there are ... endless flowers massed in carpets of varie-
gated colors. In the woods below we may find some Indian pipes, queer, colorless,
pipelike parasites which live in the moist deep woods of the west slope."
(Thompson: No. 1 on Waterton-Glacier International Peace Park map).

DEVIL'S CLUB
(Oplopanax horridus)
GINSENG FAMILY

NAME SOURCE: The genus name, *Oplopanax*, is partially derived from the Greek word *hoplon*, which means "weapon" and refers to the plant's ferocious spines. *Hoplon* is also the root of the term "Hoplite." The Hoplites were heavily armed soldiers of early Greece. The specific epithet, *horridus*, means "prickly."

DESCRIPTION: A terribly spiny shrub, it grows up to ten feet (3 m) tall, with large, maplelike leaves that become over twenty inches (52 cm) wide. It has inconspicuous greenish-white flowers. The sharp stiff spines grow from the stems, the leafstalks, and even the leaf blades. The large, lobed leaves have small marginal teeth. The flowers, each about one-fourth inch (6 mm) across, are crowded into tight buttons at the top of short stalks. In summer and fall, a conical cluster of shiny, brilliant red berries, each about three-eighths inch (9 mm) long, rises from among the leaves.

HABITAT: Moist woods, especially near streams.

SEASON: June to July.

COMMENTS: A. P. Coleman, geology professor at the University of Toronto, spent the summer of 1884 exploring the Selkirk Mountains in what is now Glacier National Park in Canada and wrote *The Canadian Rockies: New and Old Trails.* Crossing the Columbia River by raft on his way to the climb, Coleman wrote:

Even the leaf blades of devil's club has spines.

"[W]e set out through the cedars by compass, presently reaching the creek valley... Here I had my first encounter with that torment of the moister forests, the devil's club—slender, withy, and graceful, but the most diabolical plant in America, lurking among the ferns to fill one's hands with poisonous needles."

In *Among the Selkirk Glaciers*, Reverend William Green likewise recounted his 1888 cross-country hike in the same park. He and a companion were approaching Mt. Bonney, "fully prepared for a hot and hard struggle.... Besides the noble pines in the prime of life, dressed with lichens, the young trees growing up, the thickets of blueberry bushes, rhododendrons and the devil's club with its long broad leaves and coral red fruit, but most terrible thorns, there is a network of fallen trees, some rotting on the ground, others piled on top of these at every possible angle, with stumps of broken branches sticking out like spikes...Sometimes a fallen log leads in the right direction, and you can walk along it, if the rotten bark does not give way and deposit you in a bed of devil's club" (Green: No. 5 on Glacier National Park map).

In his time, Conrad Kain was one of the best climbers and guides in the Canadian Rockies. In *Where the Clouds Can Go*, he commented on the approach hike to Avalanche

Devil's club has a conical cluster of shiny, brilliant red berries.

Mountain in Canada's Glacier National Park in 1909 that the devil's club is "cursed by every explorer or hunter on account of its almost invisible little thorns which pierce the skin at once." The best remedy? "Wash at once with hot water" (Kain: No. 6 on Glacier National Park map).

In *The Glittering Mountains of Canada,* J. Monroe Thorington recounted his summer climbing activities in the Canadian Rockies in 1922–1924. In the final year, he attempted but failed to climb Mt. Robson, the highest peak in the Canadian Rockies. As to the hike to the base of Mt. Robson: "The trail is unforgettable in its beauty, with spruce and cedar trees straight and perfect above a carpet of berries, fern-brakes, and devil's club; tropically luxuriant. The stream descends in cascades and rapids, with the southern cliffs of Robson almost above one's head.…Turning a corner we come out on the shore of Kinney Lake.…Just now there is not a cloud to relieve the deep blue of the sky, nor a ripple on the lake to disturb the images of tall trees and soaring peaks." (Thorington: No. 7 on Jasper National Park map).

ROUND-LEAVED ORCHID
(*Orchis rotundifolia*)
ORCHID FAMILY

OTHER NAMES: One-leaf orchis.

NAME SOURCE: The genus name, *Orchis*, is from the Greek word *orkhis*, which means "testicle" and refers to the shape of the plant's tuberous roots. The specific epithet, *rotundifolia*, means "round-leaf," the shape of the plant's one leaf.

DESCRIPTION: An erect plant, eight to twelve inches (20–30 cm) tall, with one round leaf at the base of an otherwise leafless solitary stem, it ends in a loose raceme of two to eight very showy, small, white-pink flowers. A prominent purple-spotted lip distinguishes each flower. The small delicate flowers grow in a raceme that is up to three and one-half inches (9 cm) long. Each flower is about one-half inch (13 mm) long, with petals smaller than the sepals. The purple-spotted white lip is about three-eighths inch (9 mm) long. Its single, dull green, round leaf is up to four inches (10 cm) long and grows at the base of the stem. Several flowering stems sometimes grow in a cluster.

HABITAT: Moist, cool forests.

SEASON: June to July.

COMMENTS: In ancient times it was thought that orchids were a powerful aphrodisiac because of their roots' resemblance to testicles, and that men who ate the roots would produce male children. There are around 100 species in the genus *Orchis*. The round-leafed orchid is the only one that grows in the Rocky Mountain region. Upon close inspection, the flower appears to resemble a clown or an elf.

Mt. Assiniboine, the Matterhorn of the Canadian Rockies, is about sixteen miles southwest of Banff as the crow flies, but it wasn't until 1893 that the first white men reached its base. Lawrence Burpee, in his book *Among the Canadian Alps*, wrote about one of the early trips to Assiniboine by way of Healy Creek and Simpson Pass. In this passage, he described what those early explorers found at Simpson Pass: "At the summit the snow drifts were fifteen or twenty feet deep, though it was the month of July, but as they turned down the southerly slope the snow disappeared and in its place appeared immense banks of white anemones and yellow Alpine lilies. The mossy

woods through which the trail led them the previous day had been carpeted with round-leafed orchid, with here and there a nodding Calypso [orchid], one of the most daintily beautiful and fragrant of the mountain flowers" (Burpee: No. 11 on Banff National Park map).

The round-leaved orchid is the only member of its genus that grows in the Rocky Mountain region.

LOUSEWORT
(Pedicularis contorta)

FIGWORT FAMILY

OTHER NAMES: Parrot's beak, coiled lousewort.

NAME SOURCE: The genus name, *Pedicularis*, is from the Latin word *pediculus*, which means "louse." It was believed sheep became infested with lice when grazing in a field where this plant grew. The specific epithet, *contorta*, means "twisted" and refers to the beaklike upper lip of the flower.

Lousewort is partially parasitic on the roots of other plants.

DESCRIPTION: Growing six to twenty-four inches (15–60 cm) tall, it displays a leafy stem topped by a long raceme of creamy-white to pale yellow or magenta to purple flowers. Usually several stems grow together. The raceme is three to five inches (7.5–12.5 cm) long. Each flower has an upper lip that is arched and resembles a beaklike hook. Its fernlike leaves decrease in size up the stem. Each leaf is divided into smaller leaflets that are finely toothed.

HABITAT: Wooded areas and drier meadows in the higher parts of mountains and often in sagebrush at the edge of timber.

SEASON: July to August.

COMMENTS: Lousewort has a tendency to grow in clumps. Most species of *Pedicularis* are partially parasitic on the roots of other plants.

YAMPAH
(Perideridia gairdneri)

PARSLEY FAMILY

OTHER NAMES: False caraway, squawroot.

NAME SOURCE: The genus name, *Perideridia*, is from the Greek peri, meaning "around," and *derris*, meaning "leather coat." It is not clear what characteristic this refers to in this plant.

DESCRIPTION: Growing from tuberlike roots, the usually solitary stem, one to three and one-half feet (30–150 cm) tall, branches at the top. Each branch culminates in several dense, ball-like clusters of tiny whitish flowers. Its compound leaves are divided into very narrow grasslike leaflets, one to six inches (2.5–15 cm) long. The leaves have usually dried up and withered by the time the plant has flowered.

HABITAT: Meadows and open hillsides.

SEASON: June to August.

Yampah has ball-like clusters
of tiny whitish flowers.

COMMENTS: The entire plant has a pleasing scent, reminiscent of caraway, and is the choicest of wild edible plants. Rodents eat the tuberous roots.

One of the interpreters on the Lewis and Clark Expedition was Touissant Charbonneau, whose wife was Sacajawea, a Native American. She was about sixteen at the time of the exploration, and Lewis and Clark took her along because she was familiar with parts of the Rockies they would travel through. In May 1806, the expedition was camped near present-day Lewiston, Idaho, waiting for the snow levels to lower before crossing the Rockies on their return trip east. In his journal on May 18, 1806, Captain Clark wrote: "The Squar wife [Sacajawea] to Shabono busied herself gatherin the roots of the fenel called by the Snake Indians "Year-pah" [yampah] for the purpose of drying to eate on the Rocky mountains. Those roots are very paliatiable either fresh rosted or dried and are generally between the size of a quill and that of a mans finger and about the length of the latter."

SYRINGA
(Philadelphus lewisii)
SAXIFRAGE FAMILY

OTHER NAMES: Mock-orange.

NAME SOURCE: The genus name, *Philadelphus*, means "loving one's brother or sister" and is from the Greek words *philos*, meaning "love," and *delphos*, meaning "brother." The specific epithet, *lewisii*, commemorates Captain Meriwether Lewis (1774–1809) of the Lewis and Clark Expedition. The common name, mock-orange, derives from the practice in parts of England of substituting syringa flowers for orange blossoms in wedding bouquets.

DESCRIPTION: A many-branched shrub, it grows from three to nine feet (1–3 m) tall, with heavily veined opposite leaves and numerous large, fragrant, white flowers borne in clusters at the ends of short branches. The flowers, three-fourths inch to two inches (2–5 cm) wide, usually have four petals each, about three-fourths inch (2 cm) long. The flowers have many yellow stamens. In spring, this shrub is covered with clusters of white flowers, as many as twenty flowers per cluster. Its deciduous,

In spring, syringa is covered with clusters of white flowers,
as many as twenty flowers per cluster.

light green, ovate leaves have three prominent veins and are up to three inches (7.5 cm) long. The leaves are generally slightly toothed on the edge. The fruit of this shrub is a woody capsule.

HABITAT: Rocky slopes and open, brushy areas.

SEASON: May to July.

COMMENTS: Meriwether Lewis collected this plant by the Bitterroot River in Montana. Some Native American tribes made arrows out of the shrub's straight stems. Deer browse this shrub if other forage is not available. Syringa is the state flower of Idaho.

PASQUE FLOWER
(*Pulsatilla occidentalis*)
BUTTERCUP FAMILY

OTHER NAMES: Western anemone, windflower.

NAME SOURCE: The specific epithet, *occidentalis*, means "Western." The common name, Pasque flower, is derived from the French. *Pasque* is the French term for Easter and Passover, and the flower was so named because it blooms during those religious festivals.

DESCRIPTION: A hairy plant with gray-green, fernlike leaves and several stems, it grows eight to twenty-four inches (20–60 cm) tall, with each stem topped by a solitary, creamy white flower. The flowers are one and one-half to three inches (3.8–7.5 cm) wide and often appear before the flowering stem has achieved its maximum height. The flowers have numerous stamens and are composed of five to eight petal-like sepals that are up to one-fourth inch (6 mm) long and hairy on the back. Its mostly basal leaves are finely divided and from one and one-half to three inches (3.8–7.5 cm) wide. The plant's stems and leafstalks are silky with soft white hairs. The flowers are followed by distinctive fruiting heads—upright mops of silky hairs up to one and one-half inches (3.8 cm) long.

HABITAT: Mountain slopes and meadows.

SEASON: May to September.

COMMENTS: The Pasque flower is among the first spring mountain wildflowers to bloom. Two species of blue anemones in the region are *Pulsatilla patens* and *Pulsatilla hirsutissima*. In early European history, the anemone was associated with pain and sorrow. According to superstition, when passing by a field of anemones, you were supposed to hold your breath because the wind that blew over the flowers was poisoned.

Aldo Leopold, father of the modern conservation movement in the United States, said of the Pasque flower, "Perhaps the farmers who did not want to move out of the Sand Counties had some deep reason, rooted far back in history, for preferring to stay. I am reminded of all this every spring when the pasque-flowers bloom on every gravelly ridge. Pasques do not say much, but I infer that their preference harks back to the glacier that put the gravel there. Only gravel ridges are poor enough to offer pasques full elbow-room in April sun. They endure snows, sleets, and bitter winds for the privilege of blooming alone."

In *Enchanted Trails of Glacier Park*, Canadian writer Agnes Laut anthropomorphized the Pasque flower. Driving along today's Going-to-the-Sun Road near St. Mary's Lake, she wrote: "[Y]ou will see deer jump back into dark thicket. . . . Bluebells ring as you pass. Brown-eyed susans stare. Little monkeyflowers laugh. . . . The windflower [Pasque flower] tosses out her tresses like the Undine [female water spirit] of the cataract spray—Here I am! . . . when my tresses blow you always know winter's past, spring's here—the snow is out of the passes . . . the glaciers blooming in waterfalls" (Laut: No. 6 on Waterton-Glacier International Peace Park map).

In 1929, Mabel Williams wrote *Through the Heart of the Rockies and Selkirks*, a book aimed at the growing tourist audience for the Canadian Rockies. About the beauties of Banff National Park she wrote: "At the base of Mount Temple, like a blue flower dropped from the battlements of heaven, lies little Lake Annette, a sheer mile from the lofty summit above. Myriad of wide-eyed anemones and purple asters spangle the meadows and add to the beauty of the picture while a stray chickadee flits among the spruces trilling his cheerful little song" (Williams: No. 7 on Banff National Park map).

THIMBLEBERRY
(*Rubus parviflorus*)
ROSE FAMILY

OTHER NAMES: White-flowered raspberry.

NAME SOURCE: The specific epithet, *parviflorus*, means "small-flowered" and is not a suitable description for the flowers of the thimbleberry, which are large. We need to remember that Linnaeus, the Swedish botanist who developed the binomial system for naming plants and animals, never intended specific epithets to be descriptive.

DESCRIPTION: A thornless, erect shrub, two to four feet (60–120 cm) tall, it has shreddy brown bark and almost pure white flowers growing in terminal clusters. The three- to five-lobed leaves, up to eight inches (20 cm) broad, are green above and a lighter green beneath. They are covered with a felt of short hairs and resemble maple leaves. The five-petaled flowers are one to one and one-half inches (2.5–3.8 cm) across. Its bright red, raspberry-like fruits are hemispherical.

HABITAT: Moist places, often in partial shade, growing from low to subalpine elevations.

SEASON: May to July.

COMMENTS: It often grows in dense pure stands at the edges of woods, forming thickets. In the northern Rockies, it also thrives in the pathways of avalanches. Even though the red fruits are very tart, some people enjoy eating them. Deer browse the plant, and bear and many kinds of birds eat the fruit. Some tiny insects lay their eggs in thimbleberry stalks. When these hatch into grubs within the stalk, it can sometimes cause a large, swollen gall and make the stem grotesque in shape.

In late summer 1870, Lieutenant G. C. Doane led the military escort that guided a civilian party under the leadership of General H. D. Washburn on an exploration of the area that is now Yellowstone National Park. Doane, whose writing is emotionally bland, was one of several in the party who kept a journal of the trip. On September 5, 1870, they were in the vicinity of Yellowstone Lake. Doane wrote: "The climate and vegetable growths…are strikingly different from those of the surrounding country. The summer, though short, is quite warm, notwithstanding the elevation of the district. Rains are frequent in the spring months and the atmosphere is comparatively moist. Ferns, whorttle berries, thimbleberries, and other products of a damp climate abound, all being of diminutive growth. . . . Musquitoes and gnats are said to be numerous in the early summer, but we saw none at all. The snows of winter are very heavy, but the cold is not severe for such an altitude" (Doane: No. 5 on Yellowstone National Park map).

Thimbleberry has large, almost pure, white flowers.

In his book *Camp-Fires in the Canadian Rockies,* William T. Hornaday recounted his hiking experiences in the Canadian Rockies in late summer 1905: "Our first half-day's travel up that steep mountain-groove was spent chiefly on the northern slope. There were long stretches of 'green timber'—which means living coniferous timber, green all year round. In it the ground was covered with a velvet carpet of brown needles, and ornamented with a setting of thimbleberry bushes bearing bright crimson berries."

PRICKLY SAXIFRAGE
(*Saxifraga bronchialis* var. *austromontana*)
SAXIFRAGE FAMILY

OTHER NAMES: Yellowdot saxifrage.

NAME SOURCE: The genus name, *Saxifraga*, is from the Latin words *saxum*, meaning "rock," and *frangere*, meaning "to break." This refers to this plant's rocky habitat and the belief that it could break apart rocks.

DESCRIPTION: This is a densely matted perennial with many branching leafy stems from which grow the flowering stalks, two to six inches (5–15 cm) tall, with clusters of small, white, star-shaped flowers that are conspicuously yellow spotted when young, but turn red spotted with age. The flowers, about three-eighths inch (9 mm) wide, have five petals and ten stamens. Its narrow lance-shaped evergreen leaves are one-fourth to three-fourths inch (6–20 mm) long and have stiff hairs on their edges.

HABITAT: Cliffs, rocky slopes, rock slides, and in alpine areas.

SEASON: June to August.

COMMENTS: Prickly saxifrage makes a beautiful addition to the rock garden. There are about 300 different species in the genus Saxifrage, the largest group in the Saxifrage Family.

In the summer of 1926, F. A. MacFadden visited the Canadian Rockies to collect mosses and wrote an article entitled "British Columbia: The Bryologist's Paradise." He traveled by train, occasionally getting off for a hike into the mountains. About one such excursion, he commented: "We . . . leave the train and climb up the trail to Lake O'Hara considered by many mountaineers the loveliest in the Rockies; where mosses grow on every rock and log and bank; where the lake's shore is an unbroken band of many species of soft green hepatics [liverworts] above which stand red stemmed Saxifragas and clumps of Parnassus" (MacFadden: No. 5 on Kootenay-Yoho National Park map).

FALSE SOLOMON'S SEAL
(Smilacina racemosa)

LILY FAMILY

OTHER NAMES: False spikenard.

NAME SOURCE: The specific epithet, *racemosa*, refers to the elongated flower cluster.

DESCRIPTION: This perennial with a leafy, arching stem one to three feet (30–90 cm) tall, is topped by many tiny cream-white flowers in a raceme. It is not uncommon to find several of the flowering stems in a dense cluster. At the top of the arched stem is a dense, branched cluster, up to four inches (10 cm) long, of tiny cream-white flowers. Each small flower, about one-fourth inch (6 mm) wide, has six very short oval-shaped whitish petal-like segments. The flower has six stamens. Its arched, unbranched flowering stem has large, parallel-veined, elliptic-shaped leaves that clasp the stem. Each leaf is three to eight inches (7.5–20 cm) long and about three inches (7.5 cm) wide. The nonpoisonous fruit is a round, juicy, red berry, not recommended for eating because it is strongly purgative.

HABITAT: Damp woods and clearings.

SEASON: April to July.

COMMENTS: The flower stalk of the false Solomon's seal leaves a scar on its root each year. In the same way that you can tell a tree's age by counting the rings, each stem scar on the root of the false Solomon's seal represents one year of life. The ruffed grouse eats its red berries.

J. Norman Collie and Hugh Stutfield climbed extensively in the Canadian Rockies and the Selkirk Mountains in Canada around the turn of the nineteenth century. In their book, *Climbs and Explorations in the Canadian Rockies*, they wrote of the Asulkan Valley in present-day Glacier National Park: "The real charm of the country lies in its supremely lovely woods and valleys; and of these last the most beautiful, perhaps, is that of the Asulkan. Beyond the mountain-crests which rim the view from the bottom of this valley are vast glaciers whose meltings descend in innumerable cascades flashing, jewel-like, amid the brilliant foliage. Owing to their brilliance of colouring, the Selkirk forests, in spite of their vastness, are more cheerful than those of the Rockies; and bird and animal life is more abundant" (Collie and Stutfield: No. 3 on Glacier National Park map).

LADIES' TRESSES
(*Spiranthes romanzoffiana*)
ORCHID FAMILY

OTHER NAMES: Hooded ladies' tresses, Romanzoff's ladies' tresses, pearltwist.

NAME SOURCE: The genus name, *Spiranthes*, is from the Greek words *speira*, meaning "spiral," and *anthos*, meaning "flower," a combination that refers to the spiral arrangement of the flowers on the stem. The specific epithet, *romanzoffiana*, commemorates Prince Nicholas Romanzoff, who financed a plant-collecting expedition that went around the world in 1816–1817.

DESCRIPTION: This stiff, upright, low-growing plant, four to twenty-four inches (10–60 cm) tall, with lance-shaped leaves on the lower part of the stem, culminates in a dense spike of small, whitish-green flowers, usually arranged in three rows that spiral around the stem. The narrow lance-shaped leaves are two to ten inches (5–25 cm) long and about one-half inch (1.3 cm) wide. The flower spike is up to five inches (12.5 cm) long. The flowers of the spike are three-eighths to one-half inch (9–13 mm) long. The sepals and petals form a hood over the lip of the flower.

HABITAT: Generally found in moist open places by bogs and marshes and in moist grassy depressions.

SEASON: July to September.

COMMENTS: The flowers of the ladies' tresses are strongly scented. It is one of the more common orchids in the Rocky Mountain parks.

Frances Theodora Parsons, who wrote about her experiences hiking in the Canadian Rockies at the turn of the nineteenth century, mentions ladies' tresses in her

book, *According to the Seasons:* "Occasionally this plant becomes ambitious. Leaving the low, 'wet places' to which it is assigned by the botanists, it climbs far up the hillsides. . . . The mention or sight of this little orchid, instantly recalls that breezy upland with its far-reaching view, and its hum of eager bees, which were drinking the rare sweets of the late year from the myriad spires among which I rested on that September morning."

The flowers of ladies' tresses
are strongly scented.

FOAMFLOWER
(Tiarella unifoliata)
SAXIFRAGE FAMILY

OTHER NAMES: False mitrewort.

NAME SOURCE: The genus name, *Tiarella*, is derived from the Greek word *tiara*. A tiara is a Persian headdress, which the fruit of the foamflower resembles.

DESCRIPTION: Tiny white flowers hang in loose racemes at the tops of slender leafy stems, six to sixteen inches (15–40 cm) tall. There are often three flowers to a cluster.

The small, lacy flowers grow from a light green cuplike base and are about one-fourth inch (6 mm) wide, with five white petals and ten white stamens. Some of the stamens conspicuously protrude from the center of the flower. The indented, triangular-shaped basal leaves are about three and one-fourth inches (8.4 cm) wide and are on long leafstalks. The leaf and leafstalk decrease in size on the upper parts of the flowering stem.

HABITAT: Moist shady woods and along stream banks.

SEASON: May to August.

COMMENTS: In the 1932 issue of the *Canadian Alpine Journal*, Frederick King Butters wrote an article entitled, "The Flora of the Glacier District." It introduces the reader to some of the plants and trees that might be seen on a visit to Glacier National Park in Canada. Butters wrote: "Within the forests, except in the most heavily shaded localities, the undergrowth is extraordinarily dense. Where the trees are thickest there may be only a ground cover of creeping raspberry and dwarf dogwood everywhere interspersed with the little wood fern...and with various small herbaceous plants of which the commonest are probably the Saxifragaceous *Tiarella unifoliata* and the beautiful liliaceous queen's cup [beadlily]."

TRILLIUM
(*Trillium ovatum*)
LILY FAMILY

OTHER NAMES: Wake robin, birthroot.

NAME SOURCE: The genus name, *Trillium*, was a word made up by the Swedish botanist Linnaeus (1707–1778). He formed the word from the Latin prefix *tri*, which means "three." It is an appropriate name because everything about the plant occurs in threes. There are three leaves, sepals, and petals, six stamens, and three ribs on each berry. The specific epithet, *ovatum*, is also from the Latin and means "egg-shaped," which refers to the leaf shape. The common name, wake robin, refers to the fact that this flower blooms in early spring, around the time when the robin returns from its winter migration.

DESCRIPTION: This perennial plant boasts one large white flower on a short, erect stalk growing from the center of a whorl of three broad ovate leaves. The plant grows from a bulb and is from six to sixteen inches (15–40 cm) tall. Its leaves are two to five inches (5–12.5 cm) long and almost as broad. The solitary flower is one to two inches (2.5–5 cm) across, turning pink to purple in color as it ages.

Its other common name, wake robin, refers to the fact that this flower blooms
around the time when the robin returns from its winter migration.

HABITAT: Stream banks to open thick woods, often where it is boggy in the spring.

SEASON: Early spring to early summer, as soon as the snow melts.

COMMENTS: Trillium seeds have an appendage that is rich in oil and very attractive
to ants. The ants that carry away the seeds consume only the oily part, spreading the
seed and establishing new plants away from their parent.

VALERIAN
(*Valeriana sitchensis*)

VALERIAN FAMILY

OTHER NAMES: Sitka valerian.

NAME SOURCE: The genus name, *Valeriana*, is from the Latin word valere, meaning "to be strong," and refers to the plant's strong-smelling flowers. Crush the leaves and warm them, and they smell like rotten gym socks.

DESCRIPTION: A perennial, it becomes twelve to forty inches (30–100 cm) tall, with large, coarsely toothed leaves on a stem that terminates with many small white to pinkish flowers in nearly flat clusters. The leaves have long leafstalks that decrease in size on the upper parts of the stem. The leaves occur in opposite pairs on the stem and are divided into one to four pairs of oval to oblong-shaped leaflets.

Valerian is one of the favorite foods
of the pica (rock rabbit).

HABITAT: Moist meadows and woods.

SEASON: April to August.

COMMENTS: Most members of the genus *Valeriana* have medicinal qualities. Valerian is the source of a drug used as a nerve tonic. Valerian is one of the favorite foods of the pika (rock rabbit). Native Americans cooked the roots of some species of valerian in stone-lined pits and made soup and bread out of them.

When the curtain opens for Chekhov's play *The Anniversary*, an aged bank clerk rushes on stage and shouts, "Send someone to the chemist's for three pennyworth of valerian drops. . . . I am utterly worn out. I feel ill all over."

The Alpine Club of Canada held its 1926 meeting in Tonquin Valley in Jasper National Park. One of those who attended was F. A. MacFadden, a bryologist (botanist who studies mosses). After several days of fruitful moss collecting in the boggy areas around Amethyst Lakes, he hiked to the higher part of the surrounding terrain. MacFadden wrote: "I deserted the bogs to climb Tonquin Hill directly behind camp. I followed a little streamlet tumbling down the mountain-side through the alpine forest of Spruce and Balsam Fir. . . . Among scattered trees many flowers were blooming. Above the Paint Brush, in its many alpine hues, stood the sweet-scented Valerian, while red and yellow Columbines danced in the breeze. Walking up this colorful slope I was soon beyond the trees. . . . Rocky Mountain Heather and White Heath grew in abundance and alpine Hare-bells with their large azure bells dotted the dry hill-side. On the wind-swept summit . . . the view of the mountains and valleys on every side took all my attention . . . The Ramparts were beautiful from this vantage point, Mt. Redoubt at the eastern extremity dipping into Amethyst Lakes . . . Then I realized how long a walk it had been to camp." (MacFadden: No. 6 on Jasper National Park map).

FALSE HELLEBORE
(*Veratrum viride*)

LILY FAMILY

OTHER NAMES: Corn lily, Indian poke.

NAME SOURCE: The genus name, *Veratrum*, is from the Latin words *vere*, meaning "true," and *ater*, meaning "black," which together refer to the plant's black roots. The specific epithet, *viride*, is also from the Latin and means "green," a reference to the plant's greenish flowers.

DESCRIPTION: A large plant with an unbranched thick stem, three to six feet (90–180 cm) tall, it has large, broad, heavily veined leaves and is topped by numerous small yellowish-green flowers in a long cluster. This plant often grows in dense patches. The many tiny flowers occur in a long dense terminal cluster that is from six to twelve inches (15–30 cm) long. Each small flower in the cluster is about one-half inch (1.3 cm) wide. Its stout unbranched stem is almost totally hidden by its large leaves, which clasp the stem and are six to twelve inches (15–30 cm) long and three to six inches (7.5–15 cm) wide. The fruit is an oval-shaped capsule containing many large seeds.

HABITAT: Wet meadows in montane to subalpine areas.

SEASON: June to August, depending on the elevation.

COMMENTS: False hellebore root was officially recognized as a medicinal plant in the *United States Dispensatory* from 1820 to 1942. Its use ranged from that of an emetic to a sedative, and it was also used to treat rheumatism, lung disease, and bowel complaints, to name a few. It fell into disuse because of the high variability of its toxicity. For this reason, the plant should never be used for self-medication.

The Reverend William Green and the Reverend H. Swanzy visited the area that is now Glacier National Park in Canada in 1888. Besides their church duties, the two men were accomplished topographers. The Selkirk Mountains in Glacier Park at that time had never been mapped any distance from the trans-Canada railway that crossed the mountains via Rogers Pass. The two men spent the summer mapping as much of the area as possible. One of the plants they repeatedly encountered was the false

hellebore, which the Reverend Green described as "a most striking and characteristic plant in all these valleys, wherever the heavy forest of alder fails to establish itself." About one of their mapping trips to the Lily Glacier area, Green wrote, "The mountain side to our left was still clothed in rank sub-alpine vegetation, the large succulent-leaved veratrum viride [false hellebore] affording dense cover for the marmots and other creatures uttering shrill whistling cries of alarm" (Green and Swanzy: No. 7 on Glacier National Park map).

Veratum has large, broad heavily veined leaves.

CANADA VIOLET
(Viola canadensis)
VIOLET FAMILY

NAME SOURCE: The genus name, *Viola*, is a Latin term assigned to various sweet-smelling flowers. The specific epithet, *canadensis*, means "of Canada."

DESCRIPTION: A fairly low-growing plant, four to fourteen inches, (10–35 cm) tall, it displays heart-shaped leaves that are pointed at the tip and pretty white flowers. The flowers are at the top of short stalks that grow from the leaf axils. Its showy flowers are one-half inch to one inch (1.3–2.5 cm) wide, with all the petals being yellow at the base. Two of the flower's petals are bent upward and are gently tinged with purple on the backside, with the remaining petals having purple lines on the yellow bases. The pointed heart-shaped leaves are one to three inches (2.5–7.5 cm) long and occur on slender stalks, one inch (2.5 cm) long.

HABITAT: Moist shady woods.

SEASON: May to July.

There are more than 300 species of the genus Viola found throughout the world. This is the yellow *Viola glabella.*

COMMENTS: The young leaves and buds can be used in soups and salads, and the candied flowers are not only a visual delight but delicious as well. Many wild violets resemble a miniature garden pansy. Grouse and quail eat the seeds of violets. Wild turkey eat the tuberous roots. There are over 300 species of the genus *Viola* found around the world. They occur in the temperate zone and are found on every continent except Antarctica. Flowers of this genus are not only white but also blue, violet, and yellow.

Charles Wilson was the secretary to the British Boundary Commission, which was responsible for surveying the 49th Parallel, the boundary between the United States and Canada from Minnesota to the West Coast. He kept a diary of his four years with the survey crew for his sister Fanny, back in England. On August 24, 1860, the survey crew was working in the mountainous area in central Washington state. Wilson wrote: "There is something indescribably pleasant rambling about a mountain at such an altitude; the air sharp & clear, the magnificent panorama before the eye & a buoyant & elastic feeling both of mind & body, which is never felt elsewhere, always make me more contented & feel that after all, the world is not so bad as it is painted. One seems as it were to be drawn to the Master hand that made all that is around. I gathered a couple of violets & some heath which I got up near the snow & send to you as a memento."

BEARGRASS
(*Xerophyllum tenax*)
LILY FAMILY

OTHER NAMES: Indian basket-grass, turkey beard, squaw grass, bearlily, elkgrass, pine lily.

NAME SOURCE: The genus name, *Xerophyllum*, is from two Greek words, *xeros*, meaning "dry," and *phyllon*, meaning "leaf." This refers to the plant's dry foliage. The specific epithet, *tenax*, means "holding fast" or "tough."

DESCRIPTION: A perennial, it grows up to five feet (150 cm) tall, with basal and stem leaves ending in a conspicuous cream-white raceme. The hundreds of small flowers that comprise the large conical-shaped raceme have flat petal-like segments about three-eighths inch (9 mm) long. As is the case with all racemes, the lower flowers open first. The numerous, tough, grasslike basal leaves grow in a thick clump. They are long and only about three-eighths inch (9 mm) wide. The leaves on the light-green, stout stem are much shorter than the basal leaves. From a distance, it looks like there is but one large, white flower on a tall slender stem. With its grasslike leaves, it resembles pampas grass.

HABITAT: Open woods, clearings, and hillsides, from middle to subalpine elevations.

SEASON: Late spring to August.

COMMENTS: Small rodents and game animals, especially elk, avidly eat the flowers, stalk, and tender seed pods. It often grows in dense beautiful patches, and only flowers once every five to seven years. The basal leaves are so slick that walking uphill through a dense patch of beargrass is like walking on ice.

Because of his collecting activities, David Douglas was known to the Native Americans as the "man of grass." During his journeys, he encountered beargrass several times. On July 19, 1825, he visited a Chinook tribe. After showing off his shooting skills, he said, "In the lodge were some baskets, hats made after their own fashion, cups and pouches, of very fine workmanship; some of them made with leaves of *Xerophyllum tenax* [beargrass]." A few days later, Douglas wrote in his journal: "This very interesting plant gave me at first great pleasure when it struck my eye; in an imperfect state, being neither in flower nor seed. I look on it as certain to obtain either, but after a search of three days I had the mortification to be content with

strong plants of this year's growth, and decayed stalks and capsules of last year's growth. No seed could be found. . . . The natives call it 'Quip Quip,' and make water-tight baskets of its leaves." He finally collected seeds of the beargrass near Spokane, Washington, roughly a year later, on July 27, 1826.

Beargrass often grows in dense beautiful patches and only flowers every five to seven years.

DEATH CAMAS
(*Zigadenus venenosus*)
LILY FAMILY

OTHER NAMES: Poison camas, Ward lily, poison sego.

DESCRIPTION: This perennial has numerous cream-white flowers in a pyramidal cluster at the top of a stem eight to twelve inches (20–30 cm) tall. The long, thick, parallel-veined basal leaves are four to twelve inches (10–30 cm) long. Its egg-shaped fruits are about one-half inch (1.3 cm) long when they ripen. As the plant ages, its slightly elongated bulb buries itself deeper and deeper in the ground.

The multi-flowered stalks of death camas.

HABITAT: Dry open places and often in rocky areas.

SEASON: Early spring to mid-summer.

COMMENTS: The bulbs and seeds are very poisonous to man and livestock, although hogs are claimed to be immune.

Frank Morris, a botanist, wrote an article about his first trip to Jasper National Park in the 1920s, entitled, "Nature Lovers at Jasper." He spent several days botanizing at Pyramid Lake and described that time as "one long revel of beauty and delight." Writing further about one of the areas he explored next to the lake, Morris said: "We had apparently hit on an old clearing that slanted up the slope right to the edge of the spruce woods. Its lower half was partly obscured with thickets of willow and dogwood; these were gradually succeeded by scattered poplars which in turn gave place to a stretch of open, flowery heath; a profusion of orange lilies and creamy sprays of Zygadenus [death camas] greeted our looks. . . . For if ever a piece of fairyland came within mortal ken, it was that half-acre of forest floor that we found ourselves standing in" (Morris: No. 9 on Jasper National Park map).

The inverted flowers of the yellow columbine (*Aquilegia flavescens*) resemble a group of doves.

Yellow Flowers

WE HAD SLEPT ON THE HOAR-FROSTED GRASS OF MOUNTAIN MEADOWS NEAR THE SKY; WE HAD SLEPT AMONG THE BEAVERS...WE TRAMPED IN THE RADIANT UPPER AIR; WE TRAMPED IN THE GLOOM OF ANCIENT FORESTS....WE LISTENED ONE NIGHT TO THE COYOTES CATERWAULING IN THEIR LONELINESS.

–English writer Stephen Graham,

circa 1920

YELLOW COLUMBINE
(Aquilegia flavescens)
BUTTERCUP FAMILY

NAME SOURCE: The genus name, *Aquilegia*, is from the Latin word *aquila*, which means "eagle"; the petals of some species of *Aquilegia* resemble an eagle's claws. The specific epithet, *flavescens*, also Latin, means "to make yellow," referring to the flower color. The common name, columbine, comes from the Latin word *columbinus*, meaning "dovelike." The inverted flowers resemble a group of doves.

DESCRIPTION: A perennial plant, six to thirty-six inches (15–90 cm) tall, it has several stems with numerous basal leaves and many distinctive pale to golden-yellow nodding flowers. Its large flowers are one to three inches (2.5–7.5 cm) wide and one inch (2.5 cm) or more long, with five petals and five petal-like sepals. The long hollow spurs on the petals make the flower very distinctive and easy to identify. Many long

The blue columbine (*Aquilegia caerulea*) is
Colorado's state flower.

The long, hollow distinctive spurs on columbines
make them easy to identify,

stamens grow from the flower's center. The numerous, mostly basal leaves are usually
divided into three-lobed leaflets that are three-fourths to one inch (2–2.5 cm) long
and about that wide.

HABITAT: Moist mountain meadows to alpine slopes.

SEASON: June to August.

COMMENTS: Native Americans used boiled columbine roots to treat diarrhea and
ate its leaves in salads or as a cooked vegetable. The blue columbine, *Aquilegia caerulea*,
is the state flower of Colorado; the specific epithet, *caerulea*, means "dark blue."

In *The Rockies of Canada*, Walter Wilcox recounted his climbing exploits of the late
1880s, describing many places in the Canadian Rockies. Of the Lake Louise environs,
he wrote: "There is at this end of the lake a low and swampy shore, reeking with
surface water from cold springs, unable to escape through the clayey soil beneath.
Yellow violets and several species of anemones thrive here together with a considerable number of green orchids, and the fragrant lady's tresses, but by far the most

beautiful flower is the yellow mountain columbine, a near cousin to the scarlet variety of our eastern rock banks" (Wilcox: No. 6 on Banff National Park map).

In the early 1920s, the American poet Vachel Lindsay visited what was then Waterton-Glacier Park with the English writer Stephen Graham. They spent several weeks hiking in the park, at one point making camp near Rising Wolf Mountain. In *Tramping with a Poet in the Rockies*, Graham described the scene below them: "[W]e looked a hundred miles over the plains and saw, as it were, the whole world picked out in shadow and sunshine below. Sunset slowly advanced over it all, and with reflected rays from an unseen west the day passed serenely away. Lindsay . . . slept under the great boulder, and I smoothed out a recess at the side. I lay beside scores of daintily hooded yellow columbines and looked out to the occasional licked-sweet redness of an Indian paint brush. A chipmunk rudely squeaked at us, and as a last visitor a humming bird boomed over our heads like a night-awakened beetle. We slept serenely" (Graham: No. 2 on Waterton-Glacier International Peace Park map).

Enos Mills climbed 14,255-foot Longs Peak in Rocky Mountain National Park over 250 times all told. He once said that his most enjoyable climb was when he escorted Harriet, an eight-year-old girl, to the top. On reaching the summit, Mills asked her what she thought of it, and after some serious thought, the only thing she wondered about was where all the rocks came from. Of their descent, Mills wrote: "We searched among the boulders for the columbine. Luckily we found a beautiful specimen stalk that stood several inches higher than Harriet's head." Enos and Harriet had found the blue columbine, *Aquilegia caerulea* (Mills: No. 1 on Rocky Mountain National Park map).

The blue columbine, *Aquilegia caerulea*, was first collected in Colorado by the botanist Edwin James, a member of the U.S. government's scientific expedition in 1819–1820 to explore present-day Colorado. On July 11, 1820, while camped near the South Platte River in central Colorado, James wrote, "In an excursion from this place we collected a large species of columbine, somewhat resembling the common one of the gardens. It is heretofore unknown to the Flora of the United States, to which it forms a splendid acquisition. If it should appear not to have been described, it may receive the name of Aquilegia caerulea.... It inhabits sandy woods of pine, and spruce within the mountains, rising sometimes to the height of three feet."

HEART-LEAVED ARNICA
(*Arnica cordifolia*)
COMPOSITE FAMILY

OTHER NAMES: Leopard's bane.

NAME SOURCE: The specific epithet, *cordifolia*, means "heart-shaped leaves."

DESCRIPTION: A perennial, six to twenty-four inches (15–60 cm) tall, it has a single, slightly hairy stem that displays two to four pairs of opposite, heart-shaped, slightly hairy leaves. The stem is topped by one to three broad, showy, golden-yellow flower heads. It grows in clusters because a rhizome connects the above-ground stems. The flower head has many tiny, deep-yellow disk flowers surrounded by seven to fifteen yellow ray flowers that are each three-fourths to one inch (2–2.5 cm) long. The entire flower head is one and one-half to three and one-half inches (3.8–9 cm) wide. The heart-shaped, opposite, paired leaves are one to five inches (2.5–12.5 cm) long, with the lower pairs growing from a stalk that is one to two inches (2.5–5 cm) long. The upper pairs of leaves, attached directly to the flowering stem, are usually smaller.

HABITAT: Moist soil, usually in open coniferous woods.

SEASON: April to July.

COMMENTS: All parts of the plant have been used medicinally. The flowers are the most potent. An extract made from the flower is used to soothe the pain from sprains, bruises, and overused muscles. With its opposite leaves, it is unlike most members of the Composite Family, which have alternate leaves.

    In 1907, Mary Schaffer explored much of present-day Banff National Park by horseback. Her party was one of the first to reach Watchman Lake in the extreme northwest corner of the park. She wrote: "[W]e came to a lovely ultramarine lake about a half mile in length. From its left rose a picturesque peak [Watchman Peak], and at its head stretched a fine rock wall from mountain-side to mountain-side, with spruces nestled in the ledges. Making our way round to the right of the lake the horses were soon up to their necks in alpine flowers. Columbines nodded their yellow heads from stalks three feet tall, while deep blue larkspurs, snowy valerian, flaming castilleia [paintbrush], and golden arnicas hailed our coming with flying colours." About leaving the lake, she mused: "It was hard to go from that beautiful place to leave the little lake to the butterflies, the gophers, the ducks, the bears, and the flowers. . . . But neither our coming nor going left one ripple on her placid face; born to loneliness she would not miss us" (Schaffer: No. 9 on Banff National Park map).

ARROWLEAF BALSAMROOT
(Balsamorrhiza sagittata)
COMPOSITE FAMILY

OTHER NAMES: Bigroot, big sunflower, Mormon biscuit.

NAME SOURCE: The specific epithet, *sagittata*, means "arrowhead shaped" and refers to the shape of the leaf blades. The common name, Mormon biscuit, is from the practice of early Mormon pioneers in Utah, who ate the heart of the plant's resinous root. They learned about the edibility of the plant from Native Americans.

DESCRIPTION: A perennial with a basal cluster of large, arrow-shaped, hairy, silver-gray leaves and a leafless stem, it grows from eight to thirty-two inches (20–80 cm) tall, finishing with a solitary yellow sunflower-like head. Several stems usually grow in a cluster. The heads of many members of the Composite Family have two distinct types of flowers: tiny tubular disk flowers that are surrounded by ray flowers, which look like petals. The yellow flower head of arrowleaf balsamroot is from three to five inches (7.5–12.5 cm) wide, with numerous, mostly yellow, tiny disk flowers surrounded by eight to twenty-five brilliant ray flowers. Each ray flower is one to one and three-fourths inches (2.5–4.5 cm) long. Its silver-gray, basal, arrow-shaped leaves, four to twelve inches (10–30 cm) long and half as wide, grow on a long stalk. The

Arrowleaf balsamroot has a solitary sunflower-like head
and usually grows in clusters.

leaves are covered with fine feltlike hairs and are silvery on the underside. It grows from a deep-seated, carrot-like root.

HABITAT: Dry open ground on hillsides and flats from lowlands to mountain foothills.

SEASON: April to July.

COMMENTS: Native Americans used various parts of this plant for its food and medicinal properties. They ate the inner part of the young flower stems like celery. They baked the roots, said to be sweet tasting, in a fire pit for several days, as in the preparation of blue camas. The seeds, which look like small sunflower seeds, were eaten raw or were roasted and ground into flour. The large leaves were used as a poultice for burns; a tea made from the roots was good for several ailments. Deer and elk eat the young shoots and leaves. Bighorn sheep eat the flower heads in spring.

DOGTOOTH VIOLET
(Erythronium grandiflorium)

LILY FAMILY

OTHER NAMES: Glacier lily, troutlily, fawnlily, avalanche lily, snow lily.

NAME SOURCE: The genus name, *Erythronium*, is from the Greek word *erythro*, meaning "red." This refers to the red flowers of some species. The specific epithet, *grandiflorum*, means "large flower."

DESCRIPTION: A perennial with a leafless flowering stem, six to twelve inches (15–30 cm) tall, it usually produces a single pale yellow to golden nodding flower. It has two broadly lance-shaped, shiny basal leaves four to eight inches (10–20 cm) long. There are six stamens protruding from the center of the flower, of which the anthers are dark red, pale yellow, and sometimes white. There may be up to three flowers on the stem, but it is more common to find only one.

HABITAT: Moist stream banks to alpine mountain slopes, often near melting snow.

SEASON: March to August, depending on elevation.

COMMENTS: Ground squirrel and grizzly and black bear dig up the bulbs and eat them. Other small rodents store the bulbs as part of their winter food supply. This is one of the earliest of the spring wildflowers, appearing soon after the snow has melted. It often occurs in large patches. The bulb of the dogtooth violet was only occasionally used as a food source by Native Americans, possibly due to the difficulty of digging the deep-seated bulb. When they did collect them, they boiled or dried them for winter use.

Athabasca Pass in the Canadian Rockies was the route established by David Thompson to move furs from western to eastern Canada. He was probably the first white man to cross the pass, in January 1811. In summer 1923, J. Monroe Thorington did some climbing in the area, describing it as follows: "Rounding the shoulder of Mount Kane, [the] trail leads through evergreen timber and thickets of pussy-willow, and patches of spring snow. Crowded clusters of anemones and avalanche-lilies press up through the melting margins. In the shadow of McGillivray's Rock, with the snows of Mount Brown ahead, we enter on the Athabasca Pass...snow becomes deeper, entirely covering the trail; pack-horses, floundering at first, gradually gain confidence in their footing. A gaunt cariboo stalks up and over a nearby ridge, moving so slowly" (Thorington: No. 1 on Jasper National Park map).

Roger Toll was a charter member of the Colorado Mountain Club, formed in 1912. His mountaineering activities led to his writing the book *Mountaineering in Rocky Mountain National Park*, in 1919. From 1921 to 1929, Toll was superintendent of Rocky Mountain National Park. During those years, he actively promoted and publicized the park. About a climb he made of Mt. Alice in August 1916, Toll wrote: "[W]ith our sleeping bags [we] walked up the trail toward Thunder Lake for two hours or more, and then unrolled the bags and crawled in. The object of this night trip was to get an early start the next morning. We got [up] at dawn and after caching our sleeping bags under a rock, passed Thunder Lake and struck northward up the timbered slope, brilliant with flowers of many varieties. The large yellow lily, known as the 'dog-toothed violet,' worthy companion of the columbine, grows in profusion in this region, and during the blossoming season (July and early August) would well repay a long trip. They are abundant in many parts of Wild Basin but nowhere more plentiful than here" (Toll: No. 6 on Rocky Mountain National Park map).

YELLOWBELL
(*Fritillaria pudica*)
LILY FAMILY

OTHER NAMES: Yellow fritillary, yellow snowdrop, mission bell.

NAME SOURCE: The genus name, *Fritillaria*, is from the Latin word *fritillus*, which means "dice-box." Another species in this genus, *Fritillaria meleagris*, has spotted markings on its flowers that resemble a dice board. The specific epithet, *pudica*, is from the Latin and means "bashful." This may refer to the fact that as the plant ages, the bright yellow flower turns red.

DESCRIPTION: A perennial, three to ten inches (7.5–25 cm) tall, with several slender leaves on an unbranched stem, it has at its tip usually one bell-shaped, bright yellow flower that hangs downward. The nodding flower has six petal-like segments. Each segment is about three-fourths inch (2 cm) long, and together they form the flower, which turns reddish as it ages. The flower has six stamens. It has several narrow linear leaves growing near the middle of the unbranched stem that are two to four inches (5–20 cm) long. The edible bulb is about one inch (2.5 cm) in diameter and is covered with ricelike scales.

HABITAT: Grassy hillsides and open coniferous woods.

SEASON: April to June.

COMMENTS: Native Americans ate the bulbs either raw or cooked. They taste like potatoes when eaten raw and like rice when cooked. Bear, gopher, and ground squirrel dig up the bulbs and eat them. This is one of the earlier-blooming flowers in the Rocky Mountain region.

In 1917, Mathilde Holtz and Katherine Bemis wrote the book *Glacier National Park: Its Trails and Treasures*, which gives a thorough description of all aspects of the park at the time of their visit. On one of their backcountry trips by horseback, they made a very tricky descent of Mt. Henry near Upper Two Medicine Lake. They wrote: "We descended through all the successive zones of Alpine landscape, from the lofty mountain top covered with snow down to the deep valley that was carpeted with flowery meadows. We met with all the seasons and every variety of vegetation as we descended. Winter was far up on the steep slopes of bare gnome-trees called 'Jack' pine. Autumn reigned in the region of wild ravines and green uplands, gorgeous in wild profusion of pink and white heather, wild and wayward harebells, starry asters, red paint-brush and yellow mountain bell, seen through aisles of stunted trees, tapering cedars, and spruces bearded with grey moss. Lastly our descent lay through a thick undergrowth and fragrant forest of pine and balsam. Our horses' feet sank in the soft, springy turf. Here spring vied with summer in the rich carpet of lovely blossoms spread out around us" (Bemis and Holtz: No. 12 on the Waterton-Glacier International Peace Park map).

ST. JOHN'S WORT
(Hypericum perforatum)
HYPERICUM FAMILY

OTHER NAMES: Goatweed, Klamath weed.

NAME SOURCE: The specific epithet, *perforatum*, is from the Latin, meaning "with holes." When backlighted, the leaves appear to be full of translucent pinpricks. The common name, St. John's wort, is derived from Teutonic mythology and an ancient midsummer festival in honor of Baldur, god of the summer sun. These plants are usually in flower on June 24, a day with one of the most daylight hours in the Northern Hemisphere. This plant was dedicated to Baldur. With the adoption of the Christian calendar, June 24 became St. John the Baptist's feast day, and as a result, Baldur's pretty yellow flowers were dedicated to St. John and named St. John's wort.

DESCRIPTION: A perennial, one to three feet (30–90 cm) tall, it has several slender, leafy stems that branch at the top where the starlike, bright yellow flowers are borne in clusters. The flowers are about one inch (2.5 cm) wide and have five petals and five shorter sepals, with the petals occasionally having black dots near their tips. The numerous stamens occur in several bunches and extend well past the other flower parts. Its numerous, elliptic-shaped, opposite leaves are one-half to one and

The stamens of St. John's wort occur in several bunches and extend well past the other flower parts.

one-half inches (1.3–3.8 cm) long and grow all along the erect stem.

HABITAT: Meadows and pastures in moist to fairly dry soil.

SEASON: June to August.

COMMENTS: Many superstitions have surrounded this plant. If you gathered St. John's wort on Midsummer Eve, it would ward off evil spirits and the demons of melancholy. It was advised to hang it in windows and doorways and to always carry some in your pockets as a safeguard against witches and thunder. Different beliefs about the plant were held on the Isle of Wight. There, St. John's wort conjured up demons instead of chasing them away. It was also believed that if you stepped on this plant after dark, a ghostly horse would rise from its roots, sweep you up on its back, and gallop away with you through the entire night. Grazing animals avoid St. John's wort because of its very bitter taste.

WAYSIDE GROMWELL
(*Lithospermum ruderale*)
BORAGE FAMILY

OTHER NAMES: Puccoon.

NAME SOURCE: The genus name, *Lithospermum*, is from the Greek words *lithos*, meaning "stone," and *sperma*, meaning "seed." This refers to the plant's hard seeds.

DESCRIPTION: A plant with many leafy stems in a clump, it grows from eight to twenty-four inches (20–60 cm) tall. The small, pale yellow flowers are almost hidden amid the upper leaves. The small, five-lobed flowers are about one-third inch (8 mm) long and one-fourth to one-half inch (6–13 mm) wide. Its unbranched erect stems have numerous narrow, lance-shaped, hairy leaves that are from one and one-fourth to four inches (3.1–10 cm) long. The plant grows from a large woody taproot. The fruit is divided into four shiny nutlets. Each flower often produces only one or two nutlets.

HABITAT: Dry, open places, from low to middle elevations.

SEASON: April to June.

COMMENTS: The roots of this plant and several other species of *Lithospermum* yield a dye. Its seeds are toothlike.

BISCUIT-ROOT
(*Lomatium*)

PARSLEY FAMILY

There are about seventy-five species of *Lomatium* in North America. Many of them are very similar, so it is difficult to identify species. The description given below is a general one for the genus *Lomatium*.

OTHER NAMES: Desert parsley.

NAME SOURCE: *Lomatium* is from the Greek word *lomation*, meaning "a small border or fringe," perhaps in reference to the finely cut leaves. The common name, biscuit-root, refers to the Native American usage of the roots to make biscuits.

DESCRIPTION: Members of the genus *Lomatium* are low-growing perennials with small, usually yellow flowers, crowded into umbrella-like clusters. Most members of this genus have finely divided fernlike leaves, usually at the base of the plant. They range in size from the ground-hugging *Lomatium macrocarpum* to the large chocolate tips (*Lomatium dissectum*), which can reach a height of 30 inches (75 cm). Not all lomatiums have yellow flowers. For instance, chocolate tips has deep purple flowers and *Lomatium gormanii* has white flowers.

HABITAT: Diverse habitats, generally in rocky soil.

SEASON: April to September.

COMMENTS: Lomatiums were one of the important root crops of Native Americans. The roots were dug in the spring, just after the plant had bloomed. *Lomatium cous* was probably the most widely used and became known as "cous-root" or "cows." Some of the lomatiums make important spring forage for deer, elk, and antelope. Also, bear and small rodents dig up the roots and eat them.

Captain Clark of the Lewis and Clark Expedition wrote in his journal on May 8, 1806: "[A] root called the quawmash [camas] and cows [biscuit-root] are esteemed. The cows is a knobbed root of an irregular, rounded, not unlike the gensang. . . . this root they collect rub off a thin black rind which covers it and pounding it expose it in cakes to the sun."

On the same date, Meriwether Lewis wrote about the cous-root: "These cakes are about an inch and one-quarter thick and 6 by 18 in width when dried . . . they either eat this bread alone without any further preparation, or boil it and make a thick musilage; the latter is most common and much the most agreeable. The flavour of the root is not unlike the gensang." To make the cakes, the women would pound the root heartily. Lewis said that "the noise of their women pounding the cows root reminded me of a nail factory."

BLACK TWINBERRY
(*Lonicera involucrata*)
HONEYSUCKLE FAMILY

OTHER NAMES: Bracted honeysuckle.

NAME SOURCE: The genus name, *Lonicera*, honors the German botanist Adam Lonitzer (1528–1586). The specific epithet, *involucrata*, means the plant has an involucre, which is a ring of bracts, in this case beneath the flowers.

DESCRIPTION: A perennial shrub, two to six feet (60–180 cm) tall, it displays oval-shaped, opposite leaves and small, pale yellow flowers that generally occur in pairs at the ends of the branches. The pale yellow petals of the flowers, about one-half inch (1.3 cm) long, are joined and form a tube. Beneath the five-petaled flowers are leafy bracts from which the distinctive berries grow when the flowering stage of the plant is completed. The large, shiny black, twin berries are about three-eighths inch (9 mm) in diameter. The leafy bracts from which they grow turn reddish, making the shrub's appearance very distinctive when it is in fruit. Its opposite, oval-shaped leaves, one and one-half to six inches (3.8–15 cm) long, have a long leafstalk and are slightly hairy

This shrub is very distinctive when in fruit
with is large, shiny black twinberries.

on the underside. In good growing conditions, the leaves are dark green and leathery in texture. In poor conditions, the leaves are bright green and thin.

HABITAT: Moist woods and damp thickets.

SEASON: May to August.

COMMENTS: Native Americans claimed that eating the bitter berries would make you crazy. The black twinberry is most likely to attract your attention when fruiting. Its flowers are very tiny.

SKUNK CABBAGE
(*Lysichitum americanus*)
ARUM FAMILY

OTHER NAMES: Yellow arum.

NAME SOURCE: The genus name, *Lysichitum*, is from the Greek words *lysis*, meaning "a loosening," and *chiton*, meaning "a cloak." This refers to the spathe being released from the spadix when the fruit ripens. The specific epithet, *americanum*, means "from America." The common name, skunk cabbage, refers to the fact that all members of this family tend to produce volatile oils in the base of the inflorescence near the junction of the spathe and spadix. When flowering, the spadix rises in temperature, volatilizing the oils and attracting pollinators, often flies and other creatures seeking rotting flesh.

DESCRIPTION: A perennial with a fleshy flower spike, two to eight inches (5–20 cm) long, which is composed of many tiny, yellowish to bright yellow flowers. This flower spike is partially surrounded by a yellowish sheath that grows up to twenty inches (50 cm) tall. Both the flower spike and the yellow sheath often appear before the large oval leaves have fully developed. The large, oval, basal leaves are deeply impressed with veins and when fully grown can reach a size of two feet (60 cm) by five feet

The bad-smelling flowers attract flies that pollinate the plant.

(150 cm) long. The leafstalk is generally much shorter than the leaf blade. The small yellow flowers that make up the flower spike are only about one-eighth inch (3 mm) long. The flower spike grows from a thick, fleshy rootstalk.

HABITAT: Wet, swampy places.

SEASON: April to June.

COMMENTS: The bad-smelling flowers attract flies, which pollinate the plant. Bear and elk eat the roots.

In his journal on March 10, 1853, Henry David Thoreau wrote: "At the end of winter there is a season in which we are daily expecting spring. Methinks the first obvious evidence of spring is the pushing out of the swamp willow catkins . . . then the pushing up of the skunk-cabbage spathes."

Sir Sanford Fleming was the engineer-in-chief of surveying for the cross-Canada railway. In 1883, he traveled the proposed route. During horrible weather, he and his party managed to travel only ten miles in three days as he followed the Illecillewaet River in present-day Glacier Park in Canada. Sanford said about his trying trip through Glacier: "The walking is wretchedly bad, we made little headway, and every tree, every leaf is wet and casts off the rain. In a short time we are as drenched as the foliage. We have many fallen trees to climb over, and it is no slight matter to struggle over trees ten feet and upwards in diameter. . . . Skunk cabbage is here indigenous and is found in acres of stinking perfection. . . . We try another course, only to become entangled in a windfall of prostrate trees. The rain continues falling incessantly" (Sanford: No. 1 on the Glacier National Park map).

OREGON GRAPE
(*Mahonia aquifolium*)
BARBERRY FAMILY

OTHER NAMES: Mountain holly, mahonia.

NAME SOURCE: The genus *Mahonia* is named after the American horticulturist Bernard M'Mahon (1775–1816). The specific epithet, *aquifolium*, is the name for holly and refers to this plant's leaves.

DESCRIPTION: A creeping, dwarf shrub, four to eight inches (10–20 cm) tall, it has large evergreen leaves that bare bristle-like teeth along the edges of their leaflets and dense clusters of small, bright yellow flowers. The flower clusters are two to two and one-half inches (5–6.3 cm) long. The flowers are about one-half inch (1.3 cm) wide and have six stamens. The petals and sepals of the flowers are variable, but they do occur in sets of three. Three to seven large, evergreen, compound leaves are each divided into five to nine holly-like, ovate leaflets that have spiny margins and are one and one-fourth to three inches (3.3–7.5 cm) long. The distinct, powder-blue berries are about one-fourth inch (6 mm) in diameter. The plant has a long yellow root that grows just under the surface of the ground. New plants rise at different places along the root.

HABITAT: Open coniferous woods.

SEASON: April to June.

COMMENTS: Native Americans used the plant for food, medicine, and as a dye agent. The berries were eaten raw or made into a beverage. The crushed roots placed on a wound had antiseptic properties, and a tea made from the roots was good for kidney troubles and venereal disease. A brilliant yellow dye was obtained from the roots. The drug berberis, which is used as a bitter tonic, is obtained from the plant's roots and stems. The leaves often turn a reddish color in the fall. Deer and elk browse the plant sparingly and black bear eat the berries.

On August 26, 1858, James Hector of the Palliser Expedition was in the vicinity of the lakes that form the headwaters of the Kootenay River in Canada. In his journal he wrote, "At noon we arrived at two lakes, each several miles in extent. They

A brilliant yellow dye
is obtained from the roots.

Black bear will eat the powder-blue
berries of Oregon grape.

occupy the bottom of the valley.... The day had cleared up, and the scene where we encamped on the margin of the upper lake was fresh and charming ... when we entered the lake to bathe, we found that a few yards from the shore it had a muddy bottom that was almost unfathomable. There were a number of kingfishers flitting over these lakes, grabbing at the swarms of young trout. I now began to see many plants I had not before noticed; among them ... a large-leafed plant with the leaf like a holly and a blue grapelike berry [Oregon grape]" (Hector: No. 1 on Kootenay-Yoho National Park map).

In 1872, Sir Sanford Fleming led a party of men across the breadth of Canada, locating the best route for a trans-Canada railway. One of the members of his party was George Munro Grant, who published an account of the trip in the book *Ocean to Ocean*. On September 26, 1872, they were near the confluence of the North Thompson River and the Clearwater River, just south of present-day Wells Gray Provincial Park. Despite the miserable weather, Grant took time to observe what kinds of trees and plants were growing in the area, writing: "It rained heavily this morning [causing] the delays and discomforts that rain produces. The cotton tent weighs thrice as much.... The packs are heavier and the horses' backs are wet; and it is always a question whether or not water-proofs do the rider any good ... steady drizzle and heavy mists on the hills. . . . Cedars had entirely disappeared, and the spruce and pines were comparatively small ... a dark green prickly-leaved bush like English holly, called Oregon grape, and several grasses and plants new to us covered the ground."

CINQUEFOIL
(*Potentilla*)

ROSE FAMILY

There are about 100 species of *Potentilla* in North America, of which about thirty-five are found in the Rocky Mountain region. It is a complex genus with many hybridized species. Positive identification is often very difficult. The description below is a general one for the genus *Potentilla*.

NAME SOURCE: The genus name, *Potentilla*, is from the Latin word *potens*, which means "powerful." This refers to the medicinal properties of some species of this genus. The common name, cinquefoil, means "five-leaved," which is a common trait of most cinquefoils.

DESCRIPTION: Most members of the genus *Potentilla* have yellow, saucer-shaped flowers. The flowers usually have five petals that are rounded and often are notched. The flowers have numerous stamens. All potentillas have compound leaves, meaning that the blades are divided into smaller leaflets. The flowers of the cinquefoils might be mistaken for those of the buttercup. Cinquefoils have nonwaxy petals that are unlike the waxy flowers of the buttercups. Cinquefoils range in size from the small Hooker's potentilla (*Potentilla hookeriana*) to the shrubby cinquefoil (*Potentilla fruticosa*), which can reach a height of thirty-six inches (90 cm). There are a few red-flowered species of *Potentilla*, one of which is red potentilla (*Potentilla thurberi*).

HABITAT: A variety of habitats.

SEASON: May to August.

COMMENTS: The roots of some species of *Potentilla* are edible. When cooked, they taste like sweet potatoes or parsnips. An extract from the root of *Potentilla anserina* is used to tan leather.

BUTTERCUP
(Ranunculus)
BUTTERCUP FAMILY

There are over 300 species of *Ranunculus* that grow in the cool, temperate regions of the world. Nearly forty of these are found in the United States and Canada. Positive identification of a particular species is often very difficult. Members of the genus, however, are easily recognizable. The description given provides the general characteristics of the genus *Ranunculus.*

NAME SOURCE: The genus name, *Ranunculus*, is derived from the Latin word *rana* which means "frog" and refers to the aquatic habitat of many species. The common name, buttercup, points to the similarity between the plant's gleaming petals and a cup made of butter.

DESCRIPTION: Buttercups are easily identified by their small, glossy, waxy flowers. Most buttercups have yellow flowers, but there are a few white-flowered and pink-flowered species. The flowers grow singly on a long stalk from a leafy base. Subalpine buttercup (*Ranunculus eschscholtzii*) has one of the largest flowers of the genus *Ranunculus* found in North America. Its flower is from three-fourths to one and one-half inches (2–3.8 cm) wide. The leaves of most buttercups are smooth and rather fleshy. The flowers have numerous stamens and generally have five sepals.

HABITAT: Most grow best in moist or wet habitats; a few species are found in dry sites; several are fully aquatic.

SEASON: April to July.

COMMENTS: Buttercups are among spring's early wildflowers. In Yellowstone National Park, the sagebrush buttercup (*Ranunculus glaberrimus*) is usually the first buttercup to bloom in the spring. Be aware that *all* buttercups are poisonous when eaten raw. Many buttercups were used for external medical purposes. Their stems and leaves contain an acrid juice, and it was thought that rubbing birthmarks with buttercups would remove them.

In spring 1903, when John Burroughs, American naturalist and writer, visited Yellowstone National Park with his close friend President Theodore Roosevelt, snow was still on the ground. Burroughs noted that in the Old Faithful area, "at all the formations where the geysers are, the ground was bare over a large area. I even saw a wild flower—an early buttercup, not an inch high—in bloom. This seems to be the earliest wild flower in the Rockies. It is the only fragrant buttercup I know" (Burroughs: No. 1 on Yellowstone National Park map).

Mathilde Holtz and Katharine Bemis visited what was then known as Waterton Lakes National Park in 1916, guided on this and their many other backcountry trips by Donald, a Blackfoot Indian who had been hiking Glacier's trails since childhood. Offering a combined trail guide, history lesson, and wildflower area description, they wrote: "This seven-mile trail . . . through the woods along the stream . . . brought us to Cracker Lake. This receives its name from the fact that some years ago prospectors here had to live mainly on crackers during the winter. The lake nestles at the foot of the commanding Mt. Siyeh which rises 4,200 feet above its surface. It is a rendezvous for fishermen as trout are plentiful in its waters. Most alluring was the garden of wild flowers. The high sloping meadows were covered with gentians, forget-me-nots, asters, larkspurs, harebells, yellow buttercups, columbine, goldenrod, paint-brush, saxifrage, and heather, swaying in the

Buttercups are easily identified by
their small, glossy waxy flowers.

The leaves of most buttercups
are smooth and rather fleshy.

breeze and making the air sweet. Fields of flowers!" (Bemis and Holtz: No. 7 on Waterton-Glacier International Peace Park map).

Touring the Rockies' national parks by horseback is still a popular way to see the region. In 1916, John Willy and his son spent five days exploring newly established Rocky Mountain National Park by horseback. Willy described their second day out on the trail: "We reached Thunder Pass soon after noon, and lunched alongside snowbanks that, in their melting, send water to the Pacific and the Atlantic. Here feeders of the Colorado and the Missouri Rivers originate within a few yards of each other and, in time of deep snow, from the same source. . . . Here we saw the delicate snow buttercups growing in the snow" (Willy: No. 5 on Rocky Mountain National Park map).

STONECROP
(*Sedum stenopetalum*)
SEDUM FAMILY

NAME SOURCE: The genus name, *Sedum*, is derived from the Latin word *sedeo*, which means "to sit." This refers to the low-growing habit of the plant and the way some species grow on rocks. The specific epithet, *stenopetalum*, means "narrow-petaled," in reference to the shape of the flower's petals.

DESCRIPTION: A low-growing succulent, four to eight inches (10–20 cm) tall, it has short, narrow, basal leaves and yellow flowers growing in compact clusters at the top of the stems. Its flowers, from one-fourth to one-half inch (6–13 mm) wide, have five narrow, sharp-pointed petals. The flowers are sometimes tinged with purple. The lance-shaped leaves, one-fourth to one-half inch (6–13 mm) long, grow in tufts at the base of the flowering stem. The leaves may vary in color from green to reddish brown.

HABITAT: Rocky places.

SEASON: June to August.

Stonecrop's flowers grow in compact clusters
at the tip of the stems.

COMMENTS: There are around 450 species of *Sedum,* found almost entirely in the northern temperate zone. The pika (rock rabbit) eats this plant.

Longs Peak in Rocky Mountain National Park is named after Major Stephen Long, leader of the 1819–1820 government-sponsored scientific expedition to explore part of present-day Colorado. The botanist for the expedition was Edwin James, author of the official *Account of an Expedition from Pittsburgh to the Rocky Mountains.* On July 14, 1820, James and several other men were the first white men to climb Pikes Peak. As they approached timberline on the climb, James wrote: "The day was agreeably bright and calm. As we ascended rapidly, a manifest change of temperature was perceptible, and before we reached the outskirts of the timber, a little wind was felt from the northeast. On this part of the mountain, stone-crop, is almost the only herbaceous plant which occurs."

BUFFALOBERRY
(*Shepherdia canadensis*)
OLEASTER FAMILY

OTHER NAMES: Soapberry, soopolallie.

NAME SOURCE: The genus name, *Shepherdia*, honors the English botanist John Sheppard (1764–1836). Sheppard was the curator of the Liverpool Botanic Garden and was one of the first to be successful in raising ferns from spores. The specific epithet, *canadensis*, means "of Canada." The common name, buffaloberry, has two possible derivations. Native Americans used the plant's berry to make a sauce to flavor buffalo meat. The other derivation refers to the fondness of buffalo for the berry. The common name, soapberry, refers to the frothing characteristic of the berry when it is beaten.

DESCRIPTION: A small, thornless, spreading shrub, one to three feet (30–90 cm) tall, it has broadly lanceolate, deep green, opposite leaves and small, yellowish flowers clustered in the axils of the leaves. The tiny flowers, one-eighth to one-fourth inch (3–6 mm) wide, appear with the leaves. This shrub is dioecious, meaning the flowers are either male or female. The male and female flowers do not occur on the same shrub. The male shrub produces the pollen and the female shrub produces the brilliant red berries. Its opposite leaves are three-fourths to two inches (2–5 cm) long, and although dark green above, the underside is covered with tiny brown scales. The small, spherical-shaped, shiny red berries are about one-half inch (1.3 cm) long. The juicy berries are bitter, but edible.

HABITAT: Dry open woods to timberline.

SEASON: May to July.

COMMENTS: There are only three species of *Shepherdia*, and they occur only in North America. Black bear gorge themselves on the berries. Native Americans gathered the berries and ate them fresh or stored them for winter use. A kind of ice cream was made from the berries by placing them in a bowl with some water and then beating the mixture until it became frothy. A solution made from the bark of the buffaloberry was used for sore eyes.

The Missouri River was the main route followed by many of the explorers and hunters on their trips to the Rockies in the United States. Maximilian, the prince of

Buffaloberry has very tiny spider-like yellowish flowers.

Wied-Neuwied, collected plants along the Missouri River from St. Louis to near present-day Great Falls, Montana, in 1833 and 1834. He traveled up the river on the steamboat *Yellowstone*. On May 9, 1833, he wrote in his journal: "We passed along wild, desolate banks, partly bare, partly covered with forests, or with isolated fir trees and picturesque ravines, with dark shadows, into which the close thicket scarcely allowed the eye to penetrate. We here saw, for the first time, a plant which now became more and more common; namely the buffalo-berry-bush, with pale, bluish green, narrow leaves."

SALSIFY
(Tragopogon dubius)
COMPOSITE FAMILY

OTHER NAMES: Goatsbeard, oysterplant, goat dandelion.

NAME SOURCE: The genus name, *Tragopogon*, is from the Greek words *tragos*, meaning "goat," and *pogon*, meaning beard, a possible reference to the silky pappus. The common name, oysterplant, refers to the taste of the cooked roots.

DESCRIPTION: A perennial, sixteen to forty-eight inches (40–120 cm) tall, it has a pale yellow flower head surrounded by long slender bracts that extend beyond the flowers. The flower head is at the top of a hollow stem that has several long, narrow leaves near the base. The heads of many members of the Composite Family are composed of ray flowers and disk flowers. The salsify head is different in that its flowers are perfect, being both male and female. These are called "ligulate" flowers.

The eight to thirteen pointed green bracts around the flower head are one to two inches (2.5–5 cm) long. Its narrow leaves are from four to twelve inches (10–30 cm) long.

HABITAT: Open dry ground.

SEASON: May to August.

COMMENTS: A native of Europe, it has been cultivated there for some 2,000 years because of its edible root. The cooked roots taste like oysters or parsnips. When cut, the stem yields a milky juice said to be a cure for indigestion; when the juice is mixed with mother's milk, it is reputed to be a cure for eye disorders.

On March 1, 1872, Yellowstone National Park became the first national park established in the United States. One of the men who worked hard to achieve this was Nathaniel Langford. He was part of a group of men who visited the area in the late summer of 1870. While the men were camped beneath present-day National Park

Salsify has large, round beautiful seedheads easily dispersed by the wind.

Mountain and sitting around their campfire, they discussed the idea of creating a national park. Langford wrote in his journal: "I do not know of any portion of our country where a National Park can be established furnishing to visitors more wonderful attractions than here. These wonders are so different from anything we have ever seen—they are so various, so extensive that the feeling in my mind from the moment they began to appear until we left them has been one of intense surprise and of incredulity. Every day spent in surveying them has revealed to me some new beauty, and now that I have left them, I begin to feel a skepticism which clothes them in a memory clouded by doubt" (Langford: No. 6 on Yellowstone National Park map).

Nodding onion (*Allium cernuum*) has a flower cluster that hangs downward.

Pink and Red
Flowers

AFTER NIGHTFALL THERE WAS A BEAUTIFUL AURORA; SOMETIMES LIKE A TENT, WITH STREAMS PRECEEDING EASTWARDS IN EVERY DIRECTION FROM A FIXED CENTRAL POINT, SOMETIMES LIKE A VERY GRAND ARCH STREAKING FROM EAST TO WEST. . . . THEN IT BECAME A MASS OF GLOWING RED, SPREADING OVER THE EASTERN SIDE OF THE HEAVENS, AND GRADUALLY PASSING TO THE SOUTH. . . . THE INDIANS BELIEVE THESE LIGHTS TO BE THE SPIRITS OF MEN DANCING IN THE SKY.

–James Carnegie,
Earl of Southesk, 1859

NODDING ONION
(*Allium cernuum*)

LILY FAMILY

OTHER NAMES: Wild onion.

NAME SOURCE: The genus name, *Allium*, is Latin and was given to a whole group of plants that includes onion, garlic, and chives. The specific epithet, *cernuum*, is also Latin and means "nodding," a reference to the plant's nodding flower cluster.

DESCRIPTION: A perennial, it has several erect, narrow, basal leaves from which rise a slender, leafless, flowering stem, four to twenty-four inches (10–60 cm) tall, that blossoms in a nodding cluster of many small pink flowers. The flowering stalk has a distinctive bend in it toward the top that makes the flower cluster hang downward. Each pink to white flower in the compact head has six oval-shaped, petal-like segments that are about one-fourth inch (6 mm) long. The six stamens are longer than the petals. Its narrow basal leaves are from two to ten inches (5–25 cm) long and are always shorter than the flowering stem. The plant grows from an edible elongated bulb about three-fourths inch (2 cm) in diameter.

HABITAT: Dry to moist soil in cool forests, open hillsides, and along ridges.

SEASON: June to August.

COMMENTS: Native Americans gathered *Allium* bulbs from spring to fall and ate the bulbs raw or used them in soups, stews, and meat dishes. Bear, ground squirrel, and marmot are among the wild animals that dig up and eat the bulbs. The ancients used all the alliums for their flavor and their medicinal and aphrodisiac qualities.

When the Lewis and Clark Expedition was near Three Forks, Montana, where the Missouri River branches into three rivers, Captain Lewis collected wild onions on July 22, 1805, as the group headed west to the Pacific Ocean: "I met with great quantities of a smal onion about the size of a musquit ball and some even larger; they were white crisp and well flavored. I geathered about half a bushel of them before the canoes arrived. I halted the party for breakfast . . . and the men also geathered considerable quantities of those onions."

James Hector of the Palliser Expedition came across the wild onion while exploring the Pipestone River in present-day Banff National Park. His journal for August 27, 1859, recorded: "Very cold this morning ... The ground was quite white with hoar-frost when we started to ascend ... a steep rocky path that led at some places close by snow ... still lying from last winter. After five miles we got above the woods,

The cluster of small pink flowers
of nodding onion.

and passed over a fine sloping prairie, with high bald mountains on either side. Plants with esculent [edible] roots were very abundant here, and many parts of the sward looked as if it had been ploughed, where the bears had been rooting them up like pigs. One spot on this prairie was found quite covered with a large species of onion in full flower, the stem of which grows to a height of 18 inches, with a root the size of a walnut" (Hector: No. 5 on Banff National Park map).

In the late 1880s, Walter Wilcox, an early visitor to Lake Minnewanka just outside Banff, Alberta, in Banff National

A meadow full of
nodding onion in bloom.

Park, described the area: "On the second day we passed the end of Devil's Lake [Lake Minnewanka] . . . Our camp was located in a meadow where innumerable wildflowers blossomed, and among them meadow rue and wild onions grew together. A few white blossoms—albinos—were mingled among the purple heads of wild onions. These and the other mountain flowers were slowly drowning under the rising waters of the lake, which was fed no doubt by underground springs from the mountains" (Wilcox: No. 10 on Banff National Park map).

KINNIKINNICK
(*Arctostaphylos uva-ursa*)

HEATH FAMILY

OTHER NAMES: Bearberry, bear's grape.

NAME SOURCE: The genus name, *Arctostaphylos*, is from the Greek words *arktos*, meaning "bear," and *staphyle*, meaning "bunch of grapes." It is interesting that the specific epithet, *uva-ursi*, is from the Latin words *uva*, meaning "bunch of grapes," and *ursi*, meaning "bear." The genus and specific epithet names for this plant mean the same thing. The name kinnikinnick is an Algonquin word meaning "that which is mixed," a possible reference to the use of its leaves in smoking mixtures.

DESCRIPTION: A small evergreen creeper that grows as a low dense mat, it is only about six inches (15 cm) high, with urn-shaped waxy pink flowers growing in nodding clusters at the ends of the reddish-brown woody stems. Three to fifteen flowers are in each cluster. This trailing, multibranched shrub has shiny, leathery leaves, one-fourth to one and one-fourth inch (6 mm–3.1 cm) long, that are oblong and widest near their blunt tips. The woody stems have reddish scaly bark and can grow to ten feet (3 m) long. The small waxy flowers are about one-fourth inch

The urn-shaped waxy pink flowers
of kinnikinnick.

Kinnikinnick has shiny
leathery leaves.

(6 mm) long. Its fruit is a bright red, smooth berry about the size of a pea. Its tough skin encloses a mealy pulp and a few seeds.

HABITAT: On dry slopes and in rocky areas, especially in poor soils.

SEASON: April to June.

COMMENTS: Kinnikinnick is common from sea level to alpine zones, which demonstrates its ability to grow in many habitats. In some places in the Rockies it is associated with ponderosoa pine (*Pinus ponderosa*) forests. Kinnikinnick was one of the plants Native Americans mixed with tobacco in their smoking mixtures, though they also smoked it straight. They ate the berries fresh or gathered and dried them for winter use. Until quite recently, kinnikinnick appeared in most of the world's pharmacopoeias. The leaves have medicinal properties and should be gathered in the fall. Drinking a tea made from the leaves supposedly has an antiseptic effect on the urinary tract. An odd side effect is that it may turn the urine bright green. Several wildlife species eat the berries, including bear and grouse. Deer and mountain sheep eat the leaves and twigs in fall and winter. There is probably no better groundcover for dry banks than kinnikinnick.

James Hector of the Palliser Expedition came upon this plant on October 31, 1857, near the Saskatchewan River in Alberta, Canada. His journal entry for the day was: "[We] rode for ten miles down the river to see the pines, and to seek for good feeding places for the horses. After passing over six miles of rich country, enter on a tract of sandhills, with a gravelly soil supporting a poor growth of grass, but in some parts covered with a dense matting of the smoking weed (Arctostaphylos uva-ursi), the bright red berries of which afford winter food for large coveys of the prairie hens."

The naturalist Enos Mills explored the Rocky Mountains, particularly in Colorado, during all seasons of the year in the late 1800s and early 1900s. While out winter mountaineering once, Mills wrote: "The scarlet berries and small, shining green leaves of the kinnickinnick gave colour and charm to many snowy places. Half buried in the snow, in sun or shadow, in niches of crags, or as wreath-like covering for the rocks, they were bright and cheerful everywhere."

CALYPSO ORCHID
(*Calypso bulbosa*)
ORCHID FAMILY

OTHER NAMES: Fairy slipper, false lady's slipper, Venus slipper, pink slipper-orchid, hider-of-the-north.

NAME SOURCE: The genus name, *Calypso*, is from the Greek word *kalypso*, meaning "she who conceals." Kalypso was the goddess of silence who entertained Odysseus on her island for seven years with promises of immortality. R. A. Salisbury, an English botanist, named the genus "Calypso" in the late 1700s because its plants grow in hidden places. The specific epithet, *bulbosa*, is Latin and means "with bulbs."

DESCRIPTION: A perennial with one basal leaf and a delicate yellow-purple to brown-purple, smooth stem, it grows four to ten inches (10–25 cm) tall, culminating in a solitary, pinkish-lavender, showy flower. The drooping flower is trimmed with yellow. It has three sepals and three petals, the central petal different from the other two as it forms a slipperlike lip, one-half to one inch (1.3–2.5 cm) long, with reddish-purple spots. Its solitary, dark green basal leaf, one and one-fourth to two and one-half inches (3.1–6.3 cm) long and about one inch (2.5 cm) wide, is oval shaped and slightly serrated along the edge. The plant grows from a marble-sized corm that has fleshy roots.

HABITAT: In humus in cool, moist coniferous forests and mossy woods and swamps.

SEASON: Early spring to early summer.

COMMENTS: Squirrels eat the plant, and its small corm is subject to attack by rodents and slugs because it grows so close to the surface. It is very fragrant, with an odor similar to the cultivated lily-of-the-valley. Picking the flower usually kills the plant because its small corm is very close to the surface, held there by very delicate roots that break at the slightest touch. The Calypso orchid is unlikely to be transplanted successfully because the plant's survival depends on its establishing a permanent relationship with a fungus in the soil. The fungus spreads through the soil, absorbing and modifying nutrients upon which both it and the orchid live. The Orchid Family is perhaps the largest in the world, containing some 20,000 species, many of which are found in tropical rain forests. Calypso orchid is the only representative of its genus in North America.

Frances Theodora Parsons, writing about her hiking experiences in the Canadian Rockies in 1902 near Banff, Alberta, said: "Calypso is a May orchid which I have not yet found growing in this part of the world [southern New York state]. But early one June I had the luck to see it flowering on the lower slopes of the Canadian Rockies; though unfortunately the majority of blossoms had been plucked from the plants in order to decorate the tables of the hotel dining-room at Banff." To repeat: picking this beautiful little flower will kill the plant.

Calypso orchid
is a very fragrant plant.

INDIAN PAINTBRUSH
(*Castilleja*)
FIGWORT FAMILY

There are about 200 species of *Castilleja*, mainly in North America. It is not a difficult genus to identify as it is very distinctive, but the individual species are often so similar they are hard to distinguish. The description given below is a general one for the genus *Castilleja*.

NAME SOURCE: The genus name, *Castilleja*, commemorates the eighteenth-century Spanish botanist Don Domingo Castilleja. The common name, paintbrush, refers to the fact that the plant looks like a ragged brush that has been dipped in paint.

The flower of paintbrush looks like a ragged brush
that has been dipped in paint.

DESCRIPTION: Most members of the genus *Castilleja* are perennials and have leafy unbranched stems culminating in a spikelike cluster of tiny inconspicuous flowers. The flower cluster is hidden by the numerous distinctive and colorful bracts that surround it. Indian paintbrush usually grows in clusters, with bracts ranging in color from yellow and orange to red and purple. Its inconspicuous tiny flowers resemble the flowers of a snapdragon. Most paintbrushes are covered with stiff hairs. They range in size from the scarlet-colored cliff paintbrush (*Castilleja rupicola*), which grows up to eight inches (20 cm) to the yellow-flowered annual paintbrush (*Castilleja exilis*), which may reach thirty-two inches (80 cm) tall.

HABITAT: A variety of habitats, to alpine elevations. Many species prefer deep, sandy soils.

SEASON: May to August.

COMMENTS: Its colorful bracts attract various pollinators. Hummingbirds are very fond of the red-colored paintbrushes. Even though the Indian paintbrush can produce its own food, it is semiparasitic, meaning that its roots tap the roots of other plants to obtain food. *Castilleja linariaefolia* is the state flower of Wyoming.

A few days after making the first ascent of Mt. Forbes in Banff National Park on August 10, 1902, James Outram headed for nearby Bush Pass to fill in some of the blank places on the topographical maps then available. He recounted his climbs and explorations in the book *In the Heart of the Canadian Rockies*. About Bush Pass, Outram wrote: "We rested and cooled off for a few minutes under the shelter of an enormous mass of detached rock, its base draped with ferns and mosses, and its crest ornamented by a little spruce growing in a tiny crevice high above. It lies beside the stream, with a picturesque waterfall hard by, and surrounded by a garden of flowers clustered in bewildering profusion and blazing brilliantly with richest colouring. I gathered thirty-two distinct kinds of flowers during the morning's tramp, without wandering from the direct line of march. The painter's-brush was gorgeous in a variety of shades from yellowish white and palest pink to flaming scarlet, the 'flame-flower' of Thoreau whose 'Scarlet tufts are growing in the green like flakes of fire.' Mingled with these prevailing sunset hues, masses of purple and gold, pure white and vivid blue, combined to form a matchless harmony of colour" (Outram: No. 1 on Banff National Park map).

In *Tramping with a Poet in the Rockies*, Stephen Graham recounted his visit to Waterton Lakes National Park in the 1920s with poet Vachel Lindsay. In the vicinity of Lower Two Medicine Lake, Graham wrote: "Our idea was to obtain a cross-section of the Rockies in their most primitive state unguided by convention.... We headed for the virgin land.... In an hour we were in the deep silence of the mountains encompassed on each side by exuberant pink larkspurs and blanket flowers and red paint-brush" (Graham: No. 11 on Waterton-Glacier International Peace Park map).

PIPSISSEWA
(Chimaphila umbellata)
WINTERGREEN FAMILY

OTHER NAMES: Prince's pine, waxflower.

NAME SOURCE: The genus name, *Chimaphila*, is from the Greek words *cheima*, meaning "winter weather," and *phileo*, meaning "loving," a reference to the plant's being evergreen. The specific epithet, *umbellata*, means "umbrella-like" and describes the shape of the plant's loose cluster of nodding flowers. Its common name, pipsissewa, is a Cree word meaning "it breaks into small pieces." The Cree drank a preparation of pipsissewa to break up kidney stones and gallstones.

DESCRIPTION: A small evergreen shrub, it grows eight to twelve inches (20–30 cm) tall, with leafy stems and clusters of three to eight nodding, waxy-pink flowers well above the uppermost stem leaves. The nodding flowers occur in loose clusters. Each flower is one-half to one inch (1.3–2.5 cm) wide, with five pink petals and ten stamens. Its numerous, lance-shaped, leathery leaves are toothed on the margins and arranged in whorls on the stem. The shiny, dark green leaves are paler on the underside and from one to three inches (2.5–7.5 cm) long. This shrub arises from a long, much-branched underground rhizome.

HABITAT: Moist coniferous woods and along mountain streams.

SEASON: June to August.

The nodding waxy-pink flowers of pipsissewa occur in loose clusters.

COMMENTS: This was an important medicinal plant to some Native American tribes. The leaves were put on eyes to alleviate smarting and a tea made from the plant was used to lessen fevers. The flowers of the pipsissewa are fragrant.

Henry David Thoreau often described plants as if they were his close friends. Writing about the pipsissewa on July 3, 1853, he noted:"The pipsissewa must have been in blossom some time. The back side of its petal, 'cream-colored, tinged with purple' which is turned toward the beholder, while the face is toward the earth, is the handsomer . . . a very pretty little chandelier of a flower, fit to adorn the forest floors."

CLARKIA
(*Clarkia pulchella*)
EVENING PRIMROSE FAMILY

OTHER NAMES: Pink fairies, deerhorn, ragged-robin, elkhorns.

NAME SOURCE: The genus name, *Clarkia*, honors Captain William Clark of the Lewis and Clark Expedition. The specific epithet, *pulchella*, is from the Latin and means "beautiful."

DESCRIPTION: An annual, six to twenty inches (15–50 cm) tall, it develops pink-lavender to rose-purple flowers, each with four deeply three-lobed petals. The petals are borne on top of an elongated ovary. Its flowers superficially resemble a cluster of miniature oak leaves, with the middle lobe of each petal approximately twice as wide as the side ones. The petals are about one inch (2.5 cm) long and one-half to one inch (1.3–2.5 cm) wide. All the floral parts occur in sets of four. The narrow alternate leaves are one to three inches (2.5–7.5 cm) long.

HABITAT: Dry open areas in forested regions, to middle elevations.

SEASON: June to mid-July.

COMMENTS: Captain Meriwether Lewis of the Lewis and Clark Expedition collected it on June 1, 1806, while camped on the Clearwater River in Idaho. The description of the plant in his journal was very lengthy and contained numerous botanical terms. He ended the description by writing, "I regret very much that the seed of this plant are not yet ripe and it is probable will not be so during my residence in this neighborhood."

In the early nineteenth century, the Royal Horticultural Society of London actively searched the world for new plants to bring back to England. The society chose David Douglas, a Scot, to explore the Pacific Northwest and collect as many plants as possible. His explorations took him from the coast of present-day Oregon through parts of Washington State and up into the Rocky Mountains of Canada. In May 1825, he was in the Columbia Gorge near present-day The Dalles, Oregon. He wrote: "From the Grand Rapids to the Great Falls the banks are steep, rocky, and in many places rugged. The hills gradually diminish in elevation, and are thinly clothed with stunted timber, the shrubs only a few feet high. We are no longer fanned by the huge pine or regaled by Populus tremuloides [aspen] for ever quivering in the breeze. As far as the eyes can stretch is one dreary waste of barren soil thinly clothed with herbage. In such places are found the beautiful Clarkia pulchella." On finding it again later further upstream on the Columbia, he said it was "an exceedingly beautiful plant" that he hoped might grow in England.

The name of this flower, Clarkia, honors Captain William Clark of the Lewis and Clark Expedition.

SHOOTING STAR
(Dodecatheon pulchellum)
PRIMROSE FAMILY

OTHER NAMES: American cowslip, birdbills, few-flowered shooting star.

NAME SOURCE: The genus name, *Dodecatheon*, is from the Greek words *dodeka*, meaning "twelve," and *theos*, meaning "god." In Greek mythology, twelve gods watched over some members of the genus *Dodecatheon*. The specific epithet, *pulchellum*, means "pretty."

DESCRIPTION: A perennial, four to twenty-four inches (10–60 cm) tall, it has basal leaves and a stem that culminates in a flower cluster of mostly nodding, purplish-lavender flowers. The flowers, one-half to one inch (1.3–2.5 cm) long, have five petals and five sepals that are sharply bent back from a yellowish ring. The flower looks like an object hurtling toward Earth. Its broadly lance-shaped basal leaves are from two to sixteen inches (5–40 cm) long and almost three times as long as they are wide.

HABITAT: Variable, from open grassy areas to stream banks to subalpine meadows.

SEASON: April to August.

COMMENTS: Elk and deer eat the plant in the spring. There are a few white species of shooting star, one of which, *Dodecatheon dentatum*, usually grows around waterfalls and stream banks.

The Scottish plant collector David Douglas thought the shooting star added grace to the greenness of spring in the American West and said it could "only be equaled by the European daisy or the common primrose."

In August 1938, Robert Marshall, one of the founders of the Wilderness Society, was exploring a valley beneath Mt. Doonerak in the Central Brooks Range in northern Alaska. He wrote:

The flowers of shooting star look like an object hurtling toward Earth.

"The main Pinnyanaktuk [River] climbed rapidly, sometimes cutting through steep dirt banks, sometimes splashing over bedrock, often tearing its way through yet unmelted snowbanks. The bluish white of the anemone profusely speckled the spagnum. Wherever I looked was the deep purple of the phlox and shooting star.... The creek roaring in the gorge below made stirring music, and every sense seemed satisfied except the sense of touch, which to my unpleasant surprise was just as much abused by mosquitoes above 3,000 feet, with the ground all excellently drained, as it had been in the boggy lowlands."

FIREWEED
(Epilobium angustifolium)
EVENING PRIMROSE FAMILY

OTHER NAMES: Great willow-herb, blooming Sally, willowweed.

NAME SOURCE: The genus name, *Epilobium*, is from the Greek words *epi*, meaning "upon," and *lobos*, meaning "pod." This refers to the petals on the top of the seed pod. The specific epithet, *angustifolium*, means "having narrow leaves." Its common name, fireweed, is derived from the plant's ability to grow so well in burnt-over forest areas.

DESCRIPTION: A perennial plant, up to six feet (1.8 m) tall, it has a leafy stem that culminates in a profusion of showy pink to purple flowers in a raceme. The usually unbranched stem is covered with many lance-shaped leaves, three to six inches (7.5–15 cm) long, dark green above and pale green with prominent veins on the underside. Its large flowers have four sepals and four petals. The petals are about three-fourths inch (2 cm) wide and one-half to three-fourths inch (1.3–2 cm) long. As in all racemes, the lower flowers bloom first. The flowers face outward, with the stigma and most of the stamens hanging down. The leaves resemble those of the willow.

Fireweed grows well in burnt-over forest areas.

HABITAT: Disturbed soils in open woods and hills, from lowlands to well into the mountains. This plant is particularly fond of logged and burnt-over forest areas.

SEASON: June to September.

COMMENTS: Fireweed is commonly found growing in spectacular dense patches. Elk, deer, grizzly bear, and livestock browse it, and hummingbirds love its flower nectar. *Epilobium latifolium* is a miniature version of this plant.

Palliser Expedition member James Hector, one of the earliest white explorers in the Canadian Rockies, was active in attempting to locate passes through the mountains for a trans-Canada railway. Today's railroad from Lake Louise to Golden follows a route he pioneered. On August 21, 1858, he was exploring the Vermilion River near Ochre Creek in present-day Kootenay National Park. Hector wrote in his diary: "We found raspberries and small fruit of different kinds very abundant near our camp, but as yet there is no marked difference in the vegetation from the east slope of the mountains. Among the burnt woods the whole surface is covered with a vigorous growth of Epilobium angustifolium [fireweed], with bright pink flowers and ragged seed-pods, scattering hairy seeds" (Hector: No. 4 on Kootenay-Yoho National Park map).

College professor A. P. Coleman chronicled his summer explorations from 1884 to 1908 in *The Canadian Rockies: New and Old Trails*. In 1893, his party was heading for Athabasca Pass in present-day Jasper National Park. After several weeks of difficult horseback travel, they reached Sunwapta Falls, where they camped. He writes, "Our camp near the junction was beside the waterfall in a canyon, which we had found the year before, and the mellow roar came soothingly to us in our blankets after a hard day with the axes." Following the Athabasca River to its junction with the Whirlpool River the next day, they traveled through a fire-ravaged valley: "Where the trees had fallen after a first burning, and had then been burnt a second time, the flats and hillsides were covered with fireweed in bloom, a splendid purplish red mantle to cover blackness and ashes" (Coleman: No. 5 on Jasper National Park map).

William T. Hornaday, director of the New York Zoological Society and chief taxidermist for the U.S. National Museum, spent the late summer and fall of 1905 hunting in the rugged area north of Fernie, British Columbia, in the Rocky Mountains. Of the fireweed, he wrote: "The apex of each timbered ridge was covered with a solid mass of great willow-herb or fireweed then in its brightest autumn tints of purple and red. The brilliant patches of color, which they painted on the mountain-side would have rejoiced the heart of an artist. This glorious plant covered nearly every mountain-side in that region during our September there."

STICKY GERANIUM
(*Geranium viscosissimum*)
GERANIUM FAMILY

OTHER NAMES: Cranesbill.

NAME SOURCE: The genus name, *Geranium*, is from the Greek word *geranos*, meaning "crane," and refers to the plant's carpels, which are long and pointed, resembling the bill of a crane. The specific epithet, *viscosissimum*, is also from the Greek and means "most sticky," a reference to the small, sticky hairs covering the plant's flowers, stem, and leaves.

DESCRIPTION: A perennial, up to two feet (60 cm) tall, it has leafy stems that are covered with small, sticky hairs. The stems branch and terminate in small clusters of large, saucer-shaped, reddish-purple flowers. The symmetrical flower has five dark-veined petals, each less than one-half inch (1.3 cm) long and about one inch (2.5 cm) wide. The flowers are also covered with small, sticky hairs, as are the leaves, which are lobed into sharply toothed segments.

HABITAT: Open woods and meadows, from low elevations up to high in the mountains. It is common in aspen groves.

Sticky geranium flowers are covered
with small, sticky hairs.

SEASON: May to August.

COMMENTS: Elk, deer, and moose eat the flowers, and bear browse the entire plant. A species very similar to sticky geranium is *Geranium richardsonii*, which has white flowers and is slightly taller.

When John Willy and his son toured Rocky Mountain National Park by horseback in 1916, their guide was Shep Husted, who had been living in that area for twenty-six years. Over his lifetime, Shep climbed Longs Peak over 200 times, and there is a lake named after him in the park. Willy wrote: "Shep Husted, the guide, is a great lover of wild flowers, and he took pleasure and pride in pointing out many varieties in bloom. . . . Among the flowers he picked for specimens were . . . monkshood; larkspur . . . elephant's trunk, so named because the flower is shaped like an elephant's head . . . the wild geranium, beds of which, turning red on Lulu Mountain, were a beautiful sight" (Willy: No. 3 on Rocky Mountain National Park map).

OLD MAN'S WHISKERS
(*Geum triflorum*)
ROSE FAMILY

OTHER NAMES: Prairie smoke, purple avens.

NAME SOURCE: The common name, old man's whiskers, describes the plant when it is fruiting. The fruit's feathery styles resemble long white whiskers.

DESCRIPTION: A reddish-stemmed perennial, six to twenty-four inches (15–60 cm) tall, with basal, fernlike leaves, it usually has three nodding pink or reddish-pink, bell-

Old man's whiskers has distinctive fernlike basal leaves.

shaped flowers at the tip of each stem. The flowers, about one-half inch (1.3 cm) long, have five pink or reddish-pink sepals joined at the base, forming the bell shape. The five cream-colored petals are almost totally hidden by the sepals. Its fernlike basal leaves, one and one-fourth to six inches (3.1–15 cm) long, are pinnately compound with deeply toothed leaflets. There are two very small leaves about midway up the stem. To varying degrees, the plant is covered with long, soft hairs. As the fruit matures, its styles become long and feathery, resembling a long white beard. The feathery plumes grow up to two inches (5 cm) long.

HABITAT: Moist to dry places, from lowlands to subalpine meadows and ridges of mountains.

SEASON: May to July.

COMMENTS: After the flowers have been pollinated, they turn upward and the plumes begin to grow. The plant's fruits are finally dispersed by the wind, with the long feathery styles acting like sails.

MOUNTAIN HOLLYHOCK
(*Iliamna rivularis*)
MALLOW FAMILY

OTHER NAMES: Maplemallow, stream-bank rose mallow.

NAME SOURCE: The specific epithet, *rivularis*, is from Latin and means "brook loving," in reference to the plant's preferred habitat.

DESCRIPTION: A perennial, from three to seven feet (90–210 cm) tall, it grows in a clump and has distinctive maplelike leaves and attractive pink to rose flowers. The flowers are found in a loose raceme at the top of the stem and in shorter racemes in the upper leaf axils. The five-petaled flowers are up to two and one-half inches (6.3 cm) wide and have many stamens that are joined at the base. As in all racemes, the lower flowers bloom first. Its leafy stems have rough-textured, maplelike leaves that have three to seven lobes and are from two to eight inches (5–20 cm) wide. The leaves decrease in size on the upper part of the stems.

HABITAT: Banks of creeks and rivers and in open areas.

SEASON: June to August.

COMMENTS: There are tiny hairs on the fruit that may cause skin irritation if touched.

BITTERROOT
(*Lewisia rediviva*)
PURSLANE FAMILY

OTHER NAMES: Redhead Louisa, Resurrection flower, rock rose, sand rose.

NAME SOURCE: The genus name, *Lewisia*, honors Captain Meriwether Lewis of the Lewis and Clark Expedition. The specific epithet, *rediviva*, is from Latin and means "to live again." There is an interesting story behind that part of its name. In 1814, Frederick Pursh wrote *North American Flora*, which describes some 3,000 plants and at the time was the most comprehensive book published on the plants of North America. One of the plants in Pursh's book was the bitterroot. Through an act of botanical piracy, he stole the actual plant that Meriwether Lewis had collected on July 1, 1806, in Montana, which was to be worked on by other botanists. When he began to write its description, he noticed that the roots still showed signs of life, even though it had been sitting in an herbarium for several years. Out of curiosity, he planted the roots and they began to grow. He was thus inspired to give this rejuvenating plant the specific epithet, *rediviva*, along with the genus name, *Lewisia*, after the first white man to collect the plant.

DESCRIPTION: A low perennial plant, one-half to two inches (1.3–5 cm) tall, it displays a solitary and large, showy, deep pink to nearly white flower on a leafless stem. Each flower, up to two and one-half inches (6.3 cm) in diameter, has twelve to eighteen sepals that are one-half to one and one-half inches (1.3–3.8 cm) long, and thirty to fifty stamens that vary in color and size. The flowers of members of the Purslane Family have no petals, but the sepals are petal-like. The small, succulent, linear basal leaves, one-half to two inches (1.3–5 cm) long, appear soon after the snow has melted in the spring and then wither before the plant flowers. The plant has carrotlike roots and narrow, cone-shaped buds.

HABITAT: Dry open rocky soil, from valleys to high ridges, among rocks and in rock crevices.

SEASON: Mid-spring to mid-summer.

COMMENTS: This plant is the state flower of Montana and gives its name to the Bitterroot Mountains, the Bitterroot Valley, and the Bitterroot River, all in Montana. The bitterroot, an excellent source of concentrated nutrition, was an important food source for some Native American tribes. The Flathead tribe, which inhabited Montana's Bitterroot Valley, had access to some of the best bitterroot digging grounds in the West. They held a First Roots Ceremony, which officially opened the root-digging and berry-picking season each spring, to ensure a good harvest of bitter-roots. They dug the root before the plant bloomed, then peeled and washed it, sometimes removing the heart, which was thought to cause the bitter taste. Roots not immediately used were kept for a year or two. A tea of the boiled roots was suppos-edly good for heart trouble and pleurisy.

    Lewis and Clark were the first white explorers to encounter the bitterroot. On August 22, 1805, near the headwaters of the Beaverhead River in the Big Hole Valley of western Montana, they had a scuffle with a small band of Native Americans, who then fled, leaving behind some belongings. Upon inspecting these items, Lewis found a root he didn't recognize. Lewis wrote: "It appeared to be fibrous. The parts were brittle, hard, and of the size of a small quill, cylindric, and white as snow throughout except some small parts of the hard black rind." This was the dried bitterroot, which Lewis tasted, but found bitter and nauseating. He finally collected the bitterroot plant itself on July 1, 1806, at the mouth of Lolo Creek near present-day Missoula, Montana.

TWINFLOWER
(Linnaea borealis)

HONEYSUCKLE FAMILY

OTHER NAMES: American twinflower.

NAME SOURCE: The genus name, *Linnaea*, commemorates the Swedish botanist Linnaeus (1707–1778). The specific epithet, *borealis*, means "northern."

DESCRIPTION: This sweet-scented, creeping plant with erect, leafless flower stalks grows less than four inches (10 cm) tall and divides into two flower stalks at the top, each bearing a single, vase-shaped pink or white nodding flower that is about one-half inch (1.3 cm) long. Its small dark green opposite leaves, one-fourth to one inch (6–25 mm) long, are oval shaped and appear to hug the ground. When this plant's evergreen leaves are young, they are extremely shiny. The flowers usually have four stamens, two of which are longer.

HABITAT: Cool, moist coniferous woods as well as dry woods, from low to high elevations.

SEASON: June to September.

COMMENTS: Bighorn sheep browse this plant and grouse eat its fruit. A large patch of twinflower, all in bloom, is quite a sight. It makes an excellent groundcover in the woodland garden. The sticky dry fruits become easily attached to the fur of animals because of their tiny hooked bristles, thus helping to spread the seeds.

Portraits of Linnaeus, after whom the plant is named, usually show him with a sprig of the twinflower, named for him, in his buttonhole. Ralph Waldo Emerson referred to this flower as the "monument of the man of flowers."

After John Muir visited Yellowstone National Park, he wrote about his experience in *Our National Parks*. About the Grand Canyon in Yellowstone, Muir

The genus of twinflower, Linnaea, honors the Swedish botanist Linnaeus (1707–1778).

wrote: "The canon is so tremendously wild and impressive that even these great falls cannot hold your attention. It is about 20 miles long and 1,000 feet deep, a weird unearthly looking gorge of jagged, fantastic architecture and most brilliantly colored. . . . It is not the depth or the shape of the canon, nor the waterfall, nor the green and grey river chanting its brave song as it goes foaming on its way, that most impresses the observer, but the colors of the decomposed volcanic rocks. . . . All the earth hereabouts seems to be paint. . . . The effect is so novel and awful, we imagine that even a river might be afraid to enter such a place. But the rich and gentle beauty of the vegetation is reassuring. The lovely Linnaea borealis [twinflower] hangs her twin bells over the brink of the cliffs, forests and gardens extend their treasures in smiling confidence on either side, nuts and berries ripen well whatever may be going on below; fears vanish, and the grand gorge seems kindly below, a beautiful part of the general harmony, full of peace and joy and good will" (Muir: No. 4 on Yellowstone National Park map).

LEWIS'S MONKEYFLOWER
(*Mimulus lewisii*)
FIGWORT FAMILY

OTHER NAMES: Monkeyflower.

NAME SOURCE: The genus name, *Mimulus*, is from the Latin word *mimus*, which means "mimic." The flowers somewhat resemble the grinning faces of monkeys. The specific epithet, *lewisii*, honors Captain Meriwether Lewis of the Lewis and Clark Expedition. Lewis collected the plant in 1806 near present-day Waterton-Glacier International Peace Park in the United States on the expedition's return trip to the East Coast.

DESCRIPTION: A perennial, one to three feet (30–90 cm) tall, it is covered with sticky hairs and has deep pink to reddish flowers blooming at the top of several leafy stems. The flowers, up to two inches (5 cm) long, are joined into five lobes that form two distinct lips. Two of the lobes form the upper lip, which bends upward, and the other three lobes bend downward and form the lower lip. The lower lip is marked with yellow patches of hair. The flowers occur singly in the axils of paired leaves at the top of the stems. Its bright green, finely toothed, lance-shaped leaves are one to four inches (2.5–10 cm) long and are opposite along the slender stems. Both stems and leaves are sticky and hairy.

HABITAT: Stream banks and open wet places, to fairly high elevations.

SEASON: June to August.

COMMENTS: Monkeyflower is one of the showiest montane flowers in Waterton-Glacier International Peace Park. It has a tendency to grow in large patches. About twenty species of *Mimulus* are found in the Rocky Mountain area. *Mimulus guttatus* is a yellow-flowered species, and *Mimulus aurantiacus* has orange flowers. *Mimulus nanus* is a dwarf monkeyflower that reaches a height of only four inches (10 cm), frequently producing only one small flower.

In *Among the Selkirk Glaciers*, the Reverend William S. Green recounted his 1888 exploration of the Selkirk Mountains in present-day Glacier National Park in Canada. Green and a companion were taking a day off prior to an attempt to climb Mt. Bonney and his companion had gone to retrieve supplies from a lower camp. Green reflected: "To be alone in this wilderness of forest and cliff, glaciers and mountain torrents, bright wild flowers, bright sunshine, and the weird cry of marmots, and with leisure to let the mind dwell on it undisturbed, was an experience well worth a day.... While he was away I was able to shoot a marmot and a little chief hare, and had them stewing for supper when he arrived. A spring of clear water, in the midst of sweet-scented, large red-flowered mimulus [monkeyflower], oozed from the rocks near our tent, and fetching water thence we made the kettle boil on the cedar logs" (Green: No. 2 on Glacier National Park map).

Monkeyflower somewhat resembles
the grinning faces of monkeys.

WOOD BETONY
(*Pedicularis bracteosa*)
FIGWORT FAMILY

OTHER NAMES: Bracted lousewort, fernleaf.

NAME SOURCE: The genus name, *Pedicularis*, is from the Latin word *pediculus*, which means "louse." It was believed that a field that had wood betony growing in it would produce lice in sheep. The specific epithet, *bracteosa*, refers to the tiny bracts on the flowering stalk.

DESCRIPTION: A perennial, one to three feet (30–90 cm) tall, it has several thick stems clustered together. Each stem has fernlike leaves, and numerous pale yellow to purplish beaklike flowers at the top on an elongated leafy, bracted, spikelike raceme.

The numerous flowers, about three-fourths inch (2 cm) long, are crowded in a dense spikelike raceme. The flowers have a narrow upper lip and a shorter lower lip, with the remaining three lobes of the flower extending forward. Its large fernlike leaves, three to ten inches (7.5–25 cm) long, are divided into narrow jagged leaflets. The upper stem and leaves are often purple.

HABITAT: Moist woods and wet meadows in the mountains.

SEASON: June to August.

Each stem of wood betony has fernlike leaves and numerous purplish, beaklike flowers.

COMMENTS: In ancient times, it was believed that betony could cure any illness. Wood betony could also drive evil spirits away if planted in a graveyard or worn in an amulet. Snakes enclosed in a circle of betony would lash themselves to death. A Roman proverb said, "Sell your coat and buy betony." Elk eat the flowering heads. There are approximately 500 species of *Pedicularis* found in the temperate regions of the world. Most of them are semiparasitic, living on the roots of other plants. For this reason, they are nearly impossible to transplant successfully.

A nice campsite in a picturesque location was relished by the early visitors to the Rocky Mountain area. The Earl of Dunraven described his campsite on the south side of Mt. Washburn in Yellowstone National Park during a visit in the mid-1870s: "The sun sank in a quiet sky; the stars shone clear, bright and steady with unwavering light; the universe rested and was at peace. The wind talked to the trees, and the pines in answer bowed their stately heads, and with a sigh of melancholy swept their gloomy branches to and fro. . . . The day had been very warm, and the air was heavy with the faint odour of autumn flowers and sweet grass, and with the strong fragrance of the resinous firs. It was almost too fine a night to waste in sleep, but slumber comes soon to tired men soothed by Nature's harmony when the elements are at rest; and unconsciousness, casting over us her mantle, quickly wrapped our senses in her dark fold." (Earl of Dunraven: No. 3 on Yellowstone National Park map).

ELEPHANT HEAD
(*Pedicularis groenlandica*)
FIGWORT FAMILY

OTHER NAMES: Pink elephants.

NAME SOURCE: The genus name, *Pedicularis*, is from the Latin word *pediculus*, meaning "louse." The specific epithet, *groenlandica*, means "of Greenland." It is not known why it is so named, because this plant does not grow in Greenland. The common name, elephant head, refers to the flower, which resembles an elephant head with the trunk raised high.

DESCRIPTION: A perennial, it grows six to twenty-four inches (15–60 cm) tall, usually with several sturdy, unbranched stems growing in a cluster. Each stem has many narrow fernlike leaves and is topped by a slender spike of reddish-purple flowers. The dense flower spike is up to ten inches (25 cm) long. The flowers are unlike any other growing in the Rockies. Each flower of the spike is about one-half inch (1.3 cm) long, not including the trunk. The numerous lance-shaped leaves are one and one-half to eight inches (3.8–20 cm) long. The leaves are divided into sharp-toothed segments, giving them a fernlike appearance.

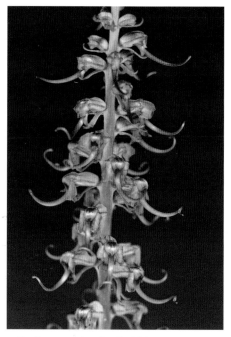

The flowers of this plant look like the tiny heads of elephants with very long tusks.

HABITAT: Moist meadows and stream margins.

SEASON: June to August.

COMMENTS: Elephant head is often found growing in large groups. Elk graze this plant in early summer.

TUFTED PHLOX
(*Phlox caespitosa*)
PHLOX FAMILY

NAME SOURCE: The genus name, *Phlox*, is from the Greek and means "a flame." Some members of the genus *Phlox* have flame-colored flowers. The specific epithet, *caespitosa*, means "to grow in dense clumps."

DESCRIPTION: A low-growing plant, two to six inches (5–15 cm) tall, it partly creeps along the ground, forming a cushionlike mat. It has closely clustered woody stems, needlelike leaves, and pretty pink flowers. The five-petaled flowers vary in color from pink to purple to white. The flowers are slightly sweet-scented and about three-fourths inch (2 cm) wide. Its numerous needlelike, narrow, opposite leaves are one-fourth to one-half inch (6–13 mm) long.

HABITAT: Dry open pine woods and sagebrush slopes.

SEASON: April to June.

COMMENTS: The genus *Phlox* is one of the most desirable genera of wildflower plants for rock gardens because of their beauty and ability to grow easily in dry conditions and places.

David Douglas mentioned the phlox in his journal entry dated May 10, 1826. At the time, he was exploring the area north of present-day Kettle Falls, Washington. His party had just survived a hair-raising experience crossing a river. After building a fire to get warm again and smoking a pipe with his Native American guide, Douglas wrote: "I continued my route till three o'clock, when I began to ascend a second ridge of mountains which I crossed and camped at dusk at their base in a thick woody valley near a small stream of water on the dry rocky ground. The small beautiful species of phlox gave the whole place a fine effect. Flower changeable, white, blue and fine pink colours."

Phlox plays a major role in this delightful passage from the novel *Cross Creek* by Marjorie Kinnan Rawlings: "The Widow Slater dressed always in a Victorian white shirtwaist and a long full-flowing black skirt. She trailed her long black skirts through the puddles of soapsuds splashed around her and carried great dripping armfuls of half-wrung sheets to the clothes line, and was concerned, not with the hardships, but with the weather and the phlox. The weather almost always suited her, for if it rained, why nothing was better for bleaching them. The phlox bothered her for the reason that they grew wild in the yard around the washbench and she was afraid of stepping on them. 'They look up at you with little faces,' she said, 'and it seemed treacherous to stomp them.'"

RED MOUNTAIN HEATHER
(*Phyllodoce empetriformis*)
HEATH FAMILY

OTHER NAMES: Heather.

DESCRIPTION: A low, matted, evergreen shrub, four to sixteen inches (10–40 cm) tall, it possesses short, stiff, needlelike leaves and numerous rose-pink, bell-shaped, nodding flowers at the ends of slender stalks. Its numerous nodding flowers grow on long, slender reddish stalks that are covered with short hairs. The petals are joined, forming a bell-shaped flower that is about three-eighths inch (9 mm) long. The needlelike evergreen leaves are about five-eighths inch (15 mm) long, each with a deep groove on the underside.

HABITAT: Rocky subalpine slopes.

SEASON: June to August.

COMMENTS: *Phyllodoce glanduliflora*, which grows together with *Phyllodoce empetriformis* in numerous places, is a similar species of mountain heather, except that it has yellowish flowers and is very hairy.

Sir George Simpson, the "Little Emperor," was one of the governors of the Hudson's Bay Company. In 1841, he made the first overland trip around the world from east to west. By year's end, as the first white man to explore the area, he was following Healy Creek in present-day Banff National Park to the pass that now bears his name. There, he and his men stopped for breakfast. Simpson wrote: "Filling our kettles for this our lonely meal at once from the crystal sources of the Columbia and the Saskatchewan ... I here met as unexpected reminiscence of my own native hills in the shape of a plant, which appears to me to be the very heather of the Highlands of Scotland . . . in all my wanderings of more than twenty years, I had never found anything of the kind in north America. . . . I carried away two specimens." It took Simpson only twelve weeks to cross North America by a route that covered 5,000 miles (Simpson: No. 4 on Banff National Park map).

In July 1923, J. Monroe Thorington and a group of men had set up their base camp in Castleguard Meadows in northwest Banff National Park after horsepacking into the area. Among their successes that summer was ascending the North Twin. Thorington described the meadows: "Here, indeed, is the spot of which wranglers dream: plenty of water, wood everywhere, horse-feed for months; and the horses can't get away! Castleguard Camp fulfills one's idea of Alpine paradise. A meadow, acres of it, with a heather carpet and flowers beyond description; little cascading streams; a tiny canyon, where leaps an arching waterfall. Can you imagine it at evening? Smoke from the campfire rising through tall trees beside the tents; horse-bell tinkling in the distance . . . the low Castleguard tongue [glacier] brilliant with light reflected from the Columbia Icefield; Mount Castleguard itself, and the Athabaska, at the valley head, old-rose and golden" (Thorington: No. 2 on Banff National Park map).

There is a white heather of the genus *Cassiope*, which was John Muir's favorite flower. The first time he encountered it was on October 3, 1869: "I had looked long and well to find its dwelling places, and began to fear that we would never meet, but had presentiment of finding it today, and as I passed a rock shelf, after reaching the great, gathered heaps of everlasting snow, something seemed to whisper, 'Cassiope, Cassiope!' That name was driven into me . . . and looking around, behold the long-looked-for mountain child."

BOG WINTERGREEN
(*Pyrola asarifolia*)
WINTERGREEN FAMILY

OTHER NAMES: Bog pyrola.

NAME SOURCE: The genus name, *Pyrola*, is from the Latin word *pyrus*, which means "pear," a reference to the shape of the plant's leaves. The specific epithet, *asarifolia*, also from Latin, means "leaves like *Asarum*," the wild ginger.

DESCRIPTION: A perennial, it grows six to eighteen inches (15–45 cm) tall, with basal leaves and deep pink to purplish-pink, cup-shaped, downward-hanging, waxy flowers in a raceme at the top of the leafless stalk. The flowers are about one-half inch (1.3 cm) wide and have five round petals that form a bowl. The flower's stigma turns down and then out and resembles an elephant's trunk. The shiny, evergreen, leathery basal leaves are oval to elliptic and are on long stalks. The leaves are about three inches (7.5 cm) long and one to three inches (2.5–7.5 cm) in diameter.

HABITAT: Moist coniferous forests of the lowlands and the mountains.

SEASON: June to August.

COMMENTS: Bog wintergreen creeps along by rhizomes just below the surface of the ground and forms extensive beds by spreading in this manner. There are several other pyrolas that grow in the Rocky Mountain area, including lesser wintergreen (*Pyrola minor*), which has small greenish-white flowers; its leaves remain green throughout the winter.

Bog wintergreen has purplish-pink, cup-shaped downward-hanging waxy flowers.

In 1880, Thomas Meehan wrote *The Native Flowers and Plants of the United States.* He commented about the leaves of the bog wintergreen: "In early spring, it is often the only living green thing among the dead leaves of the previous autumn, and serves admirably well to relieve the monotonous brown color of the forests where it loves to dwell."

In the twentieth century, Robert Marshall worked within the U.S. Forest Service developing the idea of setting aside wild areas for their wilderness value. He explored the Brooks Range in northern Alaska above the Arctic Circle in 1938. During one of his hikes, he came upon a white-flowered pyrola. He wrote: "It is hard to describe how slow and plodding it really seems when you have a 55-pound pack tugging on your headstrap and shoulders. You have hardly gone 5 minutes when the muscles in your neck are so sore that you know every step for the next 6 or 7 hours will be pain … swatting at 50 mosquitoes which have lighted on your forehead and your cheeks and your neck, letting down your black mosquito net which instantly makes the whole world dark, noticing suddenly that your ankle is sore where the boot has rubbed off the skin, stumbling over sedge tussocks, forcing your way through thick willow brush, neck aching, shoulders aching, ankle aching, on, on, on. But surprising things happen in the midst of such travel. Unexpectedly you notice a clump of lovely pyrola you almost stepped on with round, shiny leaves and stalks topped by almost bell-shaped five-petaled white flowers."

WILD ROSE
(Rosa woodsii)
ROSE FAMILY

OTHER NAMES: Coyote's berry.

NAME SOURCE: The genus name, *Rosa*, is the Latin word for the rose. The common name, coyote's berry, comes from Native American legends, in which Coyote was a hero and trickster. In one such story, Coyote came across a rosebush covered with rose hips, which he ate. As a result, his anus itched, and he scratched—to such an extent that he bled to death, thus the common name.

DESCRIPTION: A prickly shrub, two to nine feet (60–270 cm) tall, its leaves are divided into smaller, oval-shaped, sharply toothed leaflets and fairly large pink flowers. Pale pink to deep rose in color, the flowers usually occur singly all over the shrub and are up to three inches (7.5 cm) across. Each of the many-stamened flowers usually has five broad petals, one to one and one-half inches (2.5–3.8 cm) long, and five short, slender sepals. Its stem is armed with fairly short prickles. The blades, up to three inches (7.5 cm) long, are divided into five to nine oval-shaped leaflets with sharply toothed edges. The reddish, vase-shaped, smooth fruits are about three-fourths inch (2 cm) long and are commonly called rose hips.

HABITAT: Stream banks, wooded areas, and clearings.

SEASON: May to July.

COMMENTS: The short stiff hairs of the fruits enclosed in the hip were a source of "itching powder" sold in novelty stores. The fruits, called "hips," are edible and can be eaten raw or cooked as preserves. They contain a large quantity of vitamin C and ripen fully only after the first autumn frost, then remain on the shrub throughout winter. Native Americans used rose hips for both diarrhea and stomach problems. They are an important food source for ruffed grouse, quail, and small mammals; deer and elk browse the shrub. Species of *Rosa* are often difficult to identify because they hybridize so readily. The floral emblem of Alberta is the prickly rose (*Rosa acicularis*).

The Marias River enters the Missouri River about fifty miles east of Great Falls, Montana. In his journal on June 8, 1805, Meriwether Lewis of the Lewis and Clark Expedition commented, "[T]he Marias will become one of the most interesting branches of the Missouri in a commercial point of view, I have little doubt ... it passes through ... one of the most beautifully picturesque countries that I have ever beheld ... its borders garnished with one continued garden of roses."

In *The North-West Passage by Land*, Viscount Milton and W. B. Cheadle wrote an account of their trip across Canada in 1862–1863. By late June 1863, they were traveling through today's Jasper National Park, before they crossed the Continental Divide at Yellowhead Pass: "Jasper House is a neat white building, surrounded by a low palisade, standing in a perfect garden of wild flowers, which form a rich sheet of varied and brilliant colours ... In the neighborhood of Jasper House the flowers were very beautiful and various. Here grew ... an immense variety of Compositae ... roses, tiger lilies, orchids and vetches" (Milton and Cheadle: No. 2 on Jasper National Park map).

Carrie Strahorn and her husband, Robert, traveled throughout the western part of the United States from the late 1870s into the 1890s, mostly by stagecoach. Her book, *Fifteen Thousand Miles by Stage*, recounts her travels. About one of their trips in 1878, she wrote: "From Deer Lodge to Missoula [both in Montana] we forded the Deer Lodge River seven times and crossed it twice on bridges. It was a veritable Lovers' Lane leading through bowers of wild roses; oftentimes the rose bushes arched over the stage road and joined their blooms in a wealth of beauty and untrammelled luxuriance, filling the air with their fragrance and our hearts with admiration and joy. It was an expanse of earth set apart for wild growth, not only of flowers but of wild berries and wilds animals."

SPIRAEA
(Spiraea densiflora)
ROSE FAMILY

OTHER NAMES: Bridal wreath, meadowsweet.

NAME SOURCE: The specific epithet, *densiflora*, means "densely flowered."

DESCRIPTION: A multibranched shrub, two to seven feet (60–210 cm) tall, it has dense, flat-topped clusters of very tiny, pinkish flowers at the ends of the branches. Each flower has many stamens that are very conspicuous, being longer than the flower's petals. The ovate leaves are minutely toothed and about one inch (2.5 cm) long.

HABITAT: Along streams and in the moist soil of woods.

SEASON: June to July.

COMMENTS: A tea can be made from the leaves, flowers, and stems of some species of Spiraea.

The flowers of monkshood (*Aconitum columbianum*) look like hoods worn by medieval monks.

Blue and Violet
Flowers

❋

FEW, HOWEVER, THOUGHT OF PLANTS TO-DAY OR OF ANYTHING BUT THE [ROCKY] MOUNTAINS THAT STOOD IN MASSIVE GRANDEUR, THIRTY MILES AHEAD. . . .THEY ROSE BOLD AND ABRUPT FIVE OR SIX THOUSAND FEET FROM THE WOODED COUNTRY AT OUR FEET, AND FORMED IN LONG UNBROKEN LINE ACROSS OUR PATH . . .THERE WAS NO AMBIGUITY ABOUT THESE BEING MOUNTAINS, NOR WHERE THEY COMMENCED. THE LINE WAS DEFINED, AND THE SCARP AS CLEAR, AS IF THEY HAD BEEN HEWN AND CHISELLED FOR A FORTIFICATION. . . . EVERYTHING WAS IMPOSING. . . . FOR MOUNTAINS ELEVATE THE MIND, AND GIVE AN INSPIRATION OF COURAGE AND DIGNITY TO THE HARDY RACES WHO OWN THEM AND WHO BREATHE THEIR ATMOSPHERE. THE SCENE HAD ITS EFFECT ON THE WHOLE PARTY.

–Trans-Canada railway explorer
George Munro Grant, 1872

MONKSHOOD
(*Aconitum columbianum*)
BUTTERCUP FAMILY

OTHER NAMES: Aconite, wolfsbane.

NAME SOURCE: The genus name, *Aconitum*, is a Latin term used for poisonous herbs. The specific epithet, *columbianum*, means "of Columbia" and refers to the Columbia River. The common name, monkshood, refers to the shape of the flower, which looks the hood worn by medieval monks.

DESCRIPTION: A leafy perennial, it becomes two to five feet (60–150 cm) tall and culminates in hoodlike blue to purple flowers in a loose, showy, elongated flower raceme. The flowers have five blue to purple sepals, with the uppermost one forming a large hood five-eighths to one and one-fourth inch (1.5–3.1 cm) long. Two similar-colored petals are hidden under the hood. Its palmately lobed blades, two to six inches (5–15 cm) wide, are nearly circular. The leaves are distributed along the stem; the largest is at the base, and they decrease in size moving up the stem.

HABITAT: Moist places in woods to subalpine meadows, usually on stream banks.

SEASON: June to August.

COMMENTS: *Aconitum napellus* is the famous "wolfsbane" of werewolf lore. The common name, wolfsbane, came about because this plant was used to poison wolves. A strong alkaloid poison is present in the roots and leaves of all species of *Aconitum*.

On his way to attempt a climb of Mt. Brazeau in Jasper National Park in 1902, the geologist-explorer A. P. Coleman wrote about the flowers he encountered along the Saskatchewan River in Alberta: "On the passes to the north all the flowers were in blossom—white, yellow, and red heather, anemones, low buttercups, saxifrage, yellow columbine, and monk's-hood, reduced to a minimum, with one full-sized dark blue cowl on a stalk two inches high."

ASTER
(*Aster*)

COMPOSITE FAMILY

There are around 300 species of the genus *Aster* that occur in North America, and it is difficult to identify the different species. Asa Gray (1810–1888), the great American botanist, aptly summed up this difficulty when he said, "Never was so rascally a genus! They reduce me to blank despair." The description below is a general one for the genus *Aster*.

NAME SOURCE: The name *aster* is from the Latin, meaning "star," a reference to the flower's form.

DESCRIPTION: The flower heads of many members of the Composite Family are made up of two different kinds of flowers, with tiny disk flowers surrounded by larger ray flowers, each resembling a single petal. Asters are excellent examples of typical Composite heads. Members of the genus *Aster* have tiny disk flowers that range in color from red to yellow to white, and ray flowers that are blue to violet to white. Asters are perennials that are distinguished by their bicolored involucre bracts of the head. There may be one to several showy flower heads per plant. Asters range in size from the arctic aster, which has purple ray flowers and grows only four inches (10 cm) tall, to the Engelmann's aster (*Aster engelmannii*), which can grow to a height of five feet (150 cm).

HABITAT: A variety of habitats.

SEASON: Asters usually bloom in late summer after all the midsummer flowers have bloomed.

COMMENTS: The leaves, stems, and flowers of many species of asters are eaten by elk, deer, moose, and bear. It is fairly easy to distinguish asters from daisies and fleabanes if you remember that asters have bicolored involucre bracts, whereas both daisies and fleabanes have uniformly colored bracts.

George Munro Grant was a member of Sir Sanford Fleming's party, which crossed Canada in 1872, seeking the best route for a trans-Canada railway. On August 24, 1872, they were near present-day Edmonton, Alberta, heading for the Rockies. Grant wrote: "The country now became hilly; the hillsides covered with heavy marshes of lakelets. Vegetation everywhere was wonderfully luxuriant. Flowers re-appeared, but the general color was blue in place of the former yellow of lilac; mint, blue bells, a beautiful tall larkspur, but principally light and dark blue asters. Our botanist was disappointed to find that, amid such wealth of vegetation, there were few new species. The same plants have kept by us for a thousand miles."

In the late 1800s, Walter Wilcox climbed and camped throughout the Canadian Rockies. In this passage, he described the flowers in an alpine meadow near Moraine Lake: "The succession of flowering plants has reserved mid-August for the glorious climax of the floral display ... From our tent we could look over seas of untold millions of wild asters. For a quarter of a mile in every direction the dominant tone, aside from the green leaves, was a pale lilac colour, given by the innumerable delicate rayed, yellow-eyed flowers growing tall and graceful on slender stems.... Amongst them the white valerian, whose dying leaves make that strong, rank odour, noticeable everywhere in late summer, and the yellow rayed arnicas, like fallen golden stars, the painted cups and tasselled plumes of anemones were lost in sheer multitude. It seemed a pity to trample through these gardens, and so we came at length to pick our way with care" (Wilcox: No. 3 on Banff National Park map).

BLUE CAMAS
(*Camassia quamash*)
LILY FAMILY

OTHER NAMES: Wild hyacinth, camas root, quamass root, squamash, swamp sego, common camas.

NAME SOURCE: The name "camas" can be traced to the Nootka Chinook word *kamas*, meaning "sweet," a reference to its use by many Native American tribes as their main sweetening agent.

DESCRIPTION: A perennial herb one to two feet (30–60 cm) tall, it grows from an ovate bulb with an unbranched, leafless, stout stem, culminating in large, showy, star-shaped blue flowers. As with most Lily Family members, the sepals and petals are the same color and size, and all the flower parts occur in sets of three. The ovary contains three sepals, three petals, six stamens, and three compartments. The flowers are one and one-half to two and one-half inches (3.8–6.3 cm) wide and about one inch (2.5 cm) long. The several basal, grasslike leaves are one-half to three-fourths inch (1.3–2 cm) wide and about two-thirds as long as the flowering stem. The starchy bulb is about three-fourths inch (2 cm) in diameter, generally buried at least four inches (10 cm) deep.

HABITAT: Meadows and grassy flats that are moist in early spring.

SEASON: Mid-April to mid-June, depending on the elevation.

COMMENTS: The Camas Prairie, the town of Camas, Idaho, and Camas Hot Springs in Montana are named after this plant. For some Western Native American tribes, the blue camas was a significant food source.

On September 20, 1805, traveling west along Idaho's Clearwater River, Meriwether Lewis described a meal the hospitable local tribe offered them: "a small piece of buffalo meat, some dried salmon, berries and several kinds of roots . . . one which is round and much like an onion in appearance and sweet to the taste: it is called quamash, and is eaten either in its natural state, or boiled into a kind of soup or made into a cake. After the long abstinence this was a sumptous treat." On October 21, 1805, Captain Clark noted that one of their men had made some very good camas root beer. On June 12, 1806, the expedition was near present-day Orofino, Idaho, headed back east after reaching the Pacific. Lewis wrote, "[T]he quamash is now in blume and from the colour of its bloom at a short distance it resembles lakes of fine clear water . . . on first sight I could have swoarn it was water."

David Douglas, who collected plants in the Northwest in the 1820s, noted in his journal: "When warm they [cooked camas bulbs] taste like a baked pear. . . . [A]ssuredly they produce flatulence; when in the Indian hut I was almost blown out by strength of wind."

Native American women used digging sticks made of elk antler (or hawthorn, serviceberry, or other woods) to gather camas root. It was important to dig the root at its sweetest. The botanical explorer C. A. Geyer, writing in 1844, noted: "The digging of Camass takes place as soon as the lower half of the flowers on the raceme begin to fade, or better, when the time of flowering has already passed." In *Wanderings of an Artist Among the Indians of North America*, Paul Kane recounted his travels among western Canadian and U.S. tribes, describing how camas was cooked, often in combination with wild onions, "by digging a hole … then putting down a layer of hot stones, covering them with dry grass, on which the roots are placed, they are then covered with a layer of grass, and on top of this they place earth with a small hole perforated through the earth and grass down to the vegetables. Into this water is poured, which, reaching the hot stones, forms sufficient steam to completely cook the roots in a short time." Bulbs not immediately eaten were dried and stored.

Blue camas was an important food source for Native Americans.

David Thompson explored and mapped the Canadian Rockies in the early 1800s, establishing Athabasca Pass in present-day Jasper National Park as the main fur trade route over the Rockies. In his memoirs, written many years later, he noted: "A short exposure to the sun dried them [camas bulbs] sufficiently to keep for years. I have some by me which were dug up in 1811 and are now 36 years old and are in good preservation."

Nathaniel Langford visited present-day Yellowstone National Park in 1870, contributing to efforts to make Yellowstone the first U.S. national park and writing *The Discovery of Yellowstone National Park*, 1892. One of their party, Mr. Everts, got lost on September 9, 1870, while they camped near Yellowstone Lake. All searches proved futile. Langford speculated about Everts's possible survival in his diary: "If Everts has followed the stream into the Snake River Valley, he will find an abundance of camas root, which is most nutritious, and which will sustain his life." (Langford: No. 2 on Yellowstone National Park map.) After many hair-raising adventures and surviving for thirty-seven days mainly on thistle roots, Everts was found by two trappers sent out to search for him.

HAREBELL
(Campanula rotundifolia)
BELLFLOWER FAMILY

OTHER NAMES: Bellflower, Scotch bluebell, witches' thimble.

NAME SOURCE: The genus name, *Campanula*, is from Latin and means "bell," in reference to the shape of the flower. The specific epithet, *rotundifolia*, means "round-leaved" and refers to the shape of the plant's basal blades. This same plant is found in Scotland, where it is called Scotch bluebell.

DESCRIPTION: A perennial, to thirty inches (75 cm), with both basal and stem leaves, its blue-violet, bell-shaped flowers hang down from slender stems that are usually clustered. The oval to heart-shaped basal blades are usually wilted or gone by the time the plant blooms. Its stalkless stem leaves, one-half to three inches (1.3–2.5 cm) long, are very narrow. The bell-shaped, nodding flowers are three-fourths to one and one-fourth inches (2–3.1 cm) long and about three-fourths inch (2 cm) wide, with five pointed lobes that gently curve back.

HABITAT: A variety of habitats, from meadows to rocky slopes in the lowest to subalpine elevations.

SEASON: Late June to August.

COMMENTS: Blue flax (*Linum perenne* ssp. *lewisii*), with its blue, saucer-shaped flower, is sometimes confused with the harebell. A close look reveals that the petals of the blue flax are separate, whereas those of the harebell are fused.

John Muir commented on the harebell when he was climbing Glenora Peak in southeast Alaska. Muir wrote: "The harebell appears at about 4,000 feet and extends to the summit, dwarfing in stature but maintaining the size of its handsome bells until they seem to be lying loose and detached on the ground as if like snow flowers they had fallen from the sky; though frail and delicate-looking, none of its companions is more enduring or rings out the praise of beauty-loving Nature in tones more appreciable to mortals."

Both wild animals and range livestock eat the different parts of many wild plants. From his observations, the naturalist Enos Mills wrote, "Chipmunks feed upon a variety of plants. The leaves, seeds and roots are eaten. During bloom time they feast upon wild flowers. Often they make a dainty meal off the blossoms of the fringed gentian, the mariposa lily, and the harebell. Commonly, in gathering flowers, the chipmunk stands erect on hind feet, reaches up with one or both hands, bends down the stalk, leisurely eats the blossom, and then pulls down another."

CHICORY
(*Cichorium intybus*)
COMPOSITE FAMILY

OTHER NAMES: Blue sailors.

NAME SOURCE: The specific epithet, *intybus*, is from the Latin word *intubus*, meaning "wild chicory."

DESCRIPTION: A perennial, it grows one to five feet (30–150 cm) tall, with a coarse, rigid flowering stem that branches several times and has basal and stem leaves. The large dandelion-shaped blue flowers bloom along the main branches of the stem. Unlike the heads of many members of the Composite Family, which are composed of ray flowers and disk flowers, the chicory flower is made up of ligulate flowers. The pale to deep blue flower head is about two inches (5 cm) wide, and each of the ligulate flowers has five tiny teeth on the outer end. This is one of the differences between ray and ligulate flowers. Its lance-shaped basal leaves are from three to ten inches (7.5–25 cm) long and have small teeth along their margins. The leaves on the upper part of the flowering stem are smaller.

After being in full bloom in the morning, the chicory flower heads close around noon.

HABITAT: Roadsides and fields.

SEASON: April to September.

COMMENTS: The blanched leaves can be eaten in salads, and the roasted and ground roots are used as an additive to coffee. Cutting the stems yields a milky sap. This plant is actually an introduced weed. Its flower heads usually close around noon.

CLEMATIS
(*Clematis columbiana*)

BUTTERCUP FAMILY

OTHER NAMES: Purple virgin's bower, bellrue.

NAME SOURCE: The genus name, *Clematis*, is from the Greek word *klematis*, meaning "vine bianch," a reference to the plant's growth habit. The specific epithet, *columbiana*, means "of Columbia" and refers to the Columbia River.

DESCRIPTION: A vine that is up to ten feet (3 m) long, it has a solitary, bell-shaped, blue to purple to magenta flower growing all along the upper part of the stem on the leaf axils. The flowers are two to four inches (5–10 cm) in diameter and one to two and one-half inches (2.5–6.3 cm) long. They have no petals, but instead have four petal-like sepals. In the center of the flower is a rounded, compact tuft of yellow stamens. The opposite leaves are divided into three deeply lobed, ovate leaflets, each one to two and one-half inches (2.5–6.3 cm) long. Its fruits are silvery plumes that form a feathery sphere up to two and one-half inches (6.3 cm) long.

HABITAT: Dry to moist soil in woods and thickets, from the valleys to the mountains, often on steep rocky slopes.

SEASON: Early May through July.

Clematis is a vine that can grow
up to ten feet long.

COMMENTS: The feathery, plumelike styles of the dry fruits make excellent tinder. Clematis is as pretty in fruit as it is when flowering.

LARKSPUR
(Delphinium bicolor)
BUTTERCUP FAMILY

NAME SOURCE: The genus name, *Delphinium*, is derived from the Greek word *delphis*, which means "dolphin." This refers to the nectar-producing structure of the flower, which is shaped like a dolphin.

DESCRIPTION: This plant grows from thick fleshy roots and generally has an unbranched stem, six to twenty-four inches (15–60 cm) tall, with a few basal leaves. The three to ten showy bluish-purple flowers grow toward the top of the stem in a raceme. Its distinctive flowers have five large bluish-purple sepals and four inconspicuous grayish-brown petals. The sepals occur in pairs, with the fifth one being prominently spurred. The flowers are about three-fourths inch (2 cm) long and have numerous stamens. The basal leaves are roundish in shape and divided into oblong or lance-shaped segments.

HABITAT: Dry grassy slopes and meadows.

SEASON: April to July.

COMMENTS: In spring, larkspur is poisonous to cattle. Once it blooms, however, it loses some of its poisonous characteristics. Elk browse the plant in late summer and autumn.

Isabella Bird, an English lady, visited Colorado in the late summer of 1873. She related her experiences in a series of letters to her sister Henrietta in England, which were later published in *A Lady's Life in the Rocky Mountains*. Her favorite part of Colorado was Estes Park, the gateway to Rocky Mountain National Park. She was one of the first white women to climb Longs Peak. In a letter to her sister dated October 2, 1873, Isabella wrote of the flowers in the Estes Park area: "The wild flowers are gorgeous and innumerable, though their beauty, which culminates in July and August, was over before I arrived, and the recent snow flurries have finished them. The time between winter and winter is very short, and the flowery growth and blossom of a whole year are compressed into two months. Here are dandelions, buttercups, larkspurs, harebells, violets, roses, blue gentian, columbine, painter's brush, and fifty others, blue and yellow predominating; and though their blossoms are stiffened by the cold every morning, they are starring the grass and drooping over the brook long before noon, making the most of their brief lives in the sunshine" (Bird: No. 2 on Rocky Mountain National Park map).

In summer 1917, Mary Rinehart, her husband, and their three sons explored the northwestern part of the area then known as Waterton Lakes National Park by horseback. She told the story of that trip in her book, *Tenting To-Night*. Writing about the area they were traveling through on their way to Kintla Lake, Rinehart said, "[W]e were near the Flathead [River], the Kootenais on the left, the Rockies on the right, we were traveling north in a great flat basin. The meadow-lands were full of flowers. There was rather less Indian paint-brush than on the east side of the park. But there were masses everywhere of June roses, true forget-me-nots, and larkspur. And everywhere in the burnt areas was fireweed, that phoenix plant that springs up from the ashes of dead trees" (Rinehart: No. 9 on Waterton-Glacier International Peace Park map).

MOUNTAIN GENTIAN
(*Gentiana calycosa*)
GENTIAN FAMILY

OTHER NAMES: Blue gentian, pleated gentian.

NAME SOURCE: The genus *Gentiana* is named after Gentius, the king of Illyria (c. 500 B.C.), who supposedly discovered the medicinal value of the roots of the great yellow gentian (*Gentiana lutea*). The specific epithet, *calycosa*, means "cuplike" and refers to the shape of the plant's flowers.

DESCRIPTION: A perennial, four to sixteen inches (10–40 cm) tall, it usually bears only one small cup-shaped flower, deep blue to purple, per stem. The flowers are about three-fourths inch (2 cm) wide. Its opposite, ovate leaves are usually twice as wide as they are long.

HABITAT: High in the mountains, in rocky areas, stream banks, and mountain bogs.

SEASON: July through August.

COMMENTS: The fringed gentian (*Gentiana thermalis*) was adopted as the official flower of Yellowstone National Park in 1926.

John Muir praised the beauty of Yellowstone, which he visited in 1885, in *Our National Parks*, recommending that one could experience nature best by exploring it unhurriedly. An avid naturalist and a lavish writer, Muir advised readers to "Walk away quietly in any direction and taste the freedom of the mountaineer. Camp out among the grasses and gentians of glacier meadows, in craggy garden nooks ... Climb the mountains and get their good tidings. Nature's peace will flow into you as sunshine into trees. The winds will blow their own freshness into you and the storms their energy, while cares will drop off like autumn leaves."

English writer Stephen Graham and American poet Vachel Lindsay visited the area then known as Waterton Lakes National Park around 1920. In *Tramping with a Poet in the Rockies*, Graham extolled the park's natural beauty while offering myriad philosophical ramblings. Camped above timberline at the top of the Boulder Creek drainage, Graham reminisced: "We had supper that evening in a great, open mountain space, with glaciers as large as cities brooding and impending over abysses, and we looked downward to dark and gloomy rising forests gone tired on their way up towards us, and we looked upwards to the grandeur of snow-covered crags tumultuous, heaven-climbing waves of rocks. Vachel fried the beans to an accompaniment of rhythmical remarks. Poetry possessed us both. All about us was in grand, romantic, heroic strain. The carpet on which we lay was of yellow vetches and dark-blue gentians, with lichened stones interspersed" (Graham: No. 3 on Waterton-Glacier International Peace Park map).

While visiting Two Medicine Lake in what was then known as Waterton Lakes National Park, Canadian writer Agnes Laut concluded that mountain beauty was a combination of three factors: "Boundless space, a riot of color and seclusion." Flower colors moved her to write: "A paint-brush fiery as flame beside a tiger-lily, or the fire flower purpling to lavender, or the bluebell and gentian deep as pansy violet" (Laut: No. 8 on Waterton-Glacier International Peace Park map).

Alice White, a visitor to the western part of present-day Rocky Mountain National Park in 1914, the year before the park was established, wrote: "A road led from Grand Lake to Shipler Park, and we followed it all the way, through seas of flowers of every hue imaginable. The fringed blue gentians grew so thick that one swoop of the hand would have secured a large bunch, and they formed pools of blue, first on one side and then on the other side of the road" (White: No. 7 on Rocky Mountain National Park map).

WATERLEAF
(*Hydrophyllum capitatum*)
WATERLEAF FAMILY

OTHER NAMES: Woolly-breeches, dwarf waterleaf, pussyfoot cat's-breeches.

NAME SOURCE: The genus name, *Hydrophyllum*, is from the Latin words *hydro*, meaning "water," and *phyllum*, meaning "leaf," and calls attention to the watery preferences of this plant. The specific epithet, *capitatum*, means "to grow in a dense head" and refers to the shape of the flower cluster.

DESCRIPTION: A low-growing perennial, four to fourteen inches (10–35 cm) tall, it displays a small, ball-shaped inflorescence of white to blue-purple to lavender flowers growing on short stems among a few large clustered leaves. The leaves have a long leafstalk and grow from very short stems. The entire plant is slightly hairy. The numerous long stamens extend well past the sepals and petals, giving the flower cluster a distinctive bristly appearance. Growing on long leafstalks, the few large triangular-shaped blades, two to six inches (5–15 cm) long and one to five inches (2.5–12.5 cm) wide, are divided into seven to eleven leaflets. The leaves generally grow to a greater height than the ball-shaped flower cluster.

HABITAT: Rich, moist soil in open meadows and brushy areas and along shady stream banks.

SEASON: March to July.

COMMENTS: Bear, deer, and elk eat this plant. Native Americans cooked the young shoots and roots of some species of *Hydrophyllum*.

ROCKY MOUNTAIN IRIS
(*Iris missouriensis*)

IRIS FAMILY

OTHER NAMES: Western Iris, blue flag, water flag, snake lily, Western blue flag, fleur-de-lis.

NAME SOURCE: The genus name, *Iris*, means "rainbow" in Greek. Iris was the goddess of the rainbow and a member of Zeus' court. Iris so impressed Zeus with her purity that he decided to honor her forever, so he named a flower after her that would bloom in the rainbow colors of Iris's robes. The specific epithet, *missouriensis*, means "of the Missouri." This species was named by the botanist Thomas Nuttall (1786–1859). The plant was collected by his friend Nathaniel Wyeth on a cross-country trip in 1832. Wyeth found it near the source of the Missouri River, so Nuttall gave it the name *missouriensis*.

DESCRIPTION: An eight to twenty-four inch (20–60 cm) tall plant, it has several grasslike leaves at the base and usually two, but sometimes up to four, violet-blue attractive flowers at the top of the stout, nearly round stem. The showy flowers are about three to four inches (7.5–10 cm) wide and two to three inches (5–7.5 cm) long. Each flower has three downward-curving sepals that resemble petals and three petals that are erect and slightly smaller than the sepals. Both flower parts are often purple veined. Several narrow swordlike leaves grow mainly from the base. One or two of the leaves may also grow from the flowering stem and are often as long as the stem itself. The leaves are generally from eight to twenty inches (20–50 cm) long and only one-fourth to one-half inch (6–13 mm) wide. It grows and spreads from a coarse underground rhizome.

HABITAT: In meadows or in low areas where moisture is plentiful until flowering time. In summer its growing areas usually become very dry.

SEASON: May to July.

COMMENTS: Eating the seeds causes a violent burning of the mouth and throat. A bunch of it growing in one place is considered a good sign of water close to the surface. The Rocky Mountain iris has hardly any forage value to wildlife or livestock. The rootstalk contains the toxic material irisin, which acts as a violent emetic and cathartic. The iris (fleur-de-lis) is the emblem of France.

Henry David Thoreau's writings are filled with images of the flowers he encountered in his ramblings in the natural world. About an eastern member of the genus *Iris,* Thoreau wrote: "The blue flag, notwithstanding its rich furniture and its variously streaked and colored petals, is loose and coarse in its habit. How completely all character is expressed by flowers. This is a little too showy and gaudy, like some women's bonnets. Yet it belongs to the meadow and ornaments it much."

Rocky Mountain Iris has showy violet-blue flowers.

BLUE FLAX
(*Linum perenne* ssp. *lewisii*)
FLAX FAMILY

OTHER NAMES: Prairie flax.

NAME SOURCE: The genus name, *Linum*, is Latin for "flax." The specific epithet, *perenne*, means "perennial." The subspecies *lewisii* honors Captain Meriwether Lewis of the Lewis and Clark Expedition.

DESCRIPTION: A perennial, eight to thirty-two inches (20–80 cm) tall, with a mostly unbranched, slender, leafy stem, it flaunts showy, sky-blue flowers on slender stalks in loose terminal clusters. Its saucer-shaped flowers are one-half to two inches (1.3–5 cm) wide and have five petals, five sepals, and five styles that are longer than the five stamens. Each flower petal is about three-fourths inch (2 cm) long and drops soon after bloom. The numerous narrow, gray-green, alternate leaves are one-half to two inches (1.3–5 cm) long. The very slender plant stem seems to continually sway even when there is no noticeable breeze. Its shiny brown seed capsules, about one-fourth inch (6 mm) in diameter, contain oil-rich seeds.

HABITAT: Well-drained soil in prairies and meadows, to alpine elevations.

SEASON: May to September.

Blue flax has beautiful sky-blue flowers.

COMMENTS: The linen wrappings around some Egyptian mummies were made from flax. Linseed oil is obtained by crushing the seeds of *Linum usitatissimum*.

At Three Forks, Montana, the Missouri River branches into the Gallatin, Madison, and Jefferson Rivers. The Gallatin and Madison have their headwaters in Yellowstone National Park. Lewis and Clark followed the Missouri River on their western expedition. It was at Three Forks where Lewis discovered the blue flax: "The bark of the stem is thick strong, and appears as if it would make excellent flax ... if it should on experiment prove to yeald good flax and at the same time of being cut without injury to the perennial root it will be a most valuable plant."

Native Americans ate cooked blue flax seeds and made poultices of the crushed leaves for treating swellings.

In his journal entry on June 8, 1808, as he traveled through present-day British Columbia, Simon Fraser, the Canadian explorer for whom the Fraser River is named, recorded a different use for the blue flax: "Wild flax is very plenty of which the natives manufacture their thread and fishing tackle."

The trapper Osborne Russell, who in 1835 explored the Teton Valley, just south of present-day Yellowstone National Park, wrote in his *Journal of a Trapper: 1834–1843:* "[Teton Valley] was called 'Jackson Hole.' The southern part where the river enters the mountains is hilly and uneven, the whole being covered with wild sage and surrounded by high and rugged mountains upon whose summit the snow remained during the hottest months in summer. The alluvial bottoms along the river and streams intersecting it through the valley produced a luxuriant growth of vegetation, among which wild flax and a species of onion were abundant. . . . This valley, like other parts of the country abounded with game."

Father DeSmet, a Jesuit missionary from Belgium, spent much time during the mid-1800s establishing missions among the Native Americans in the Rocky Mountains. In summer 1840, he was traveling with members of the American Fur Company near Jackson, Wyoming. In *Life, Letters, and Travels of Father Pierre-Jean DeSmet,* he remembered: "In this plain as in all mountain valleys that I have traversed, flax grows in the greatest abundance; it is just the same as the flax that is cultivated in Belgium, except that it is an annual [in fact, it is a perennial]; the same stalk, calix, seed and blue flower."

LUPINE
(Lupinus)
PEA FAMILY

There are almost 200 different species of lupines growing in the United States and Canada. They are difficult to distinguish from each other in many cases, but as a genus, they are clearly distinct from most other genera in the Pea Family. The description given is a general one for the genus *Lupinus.*

NAME SOURCE: Lupines grow well in poor soil. In Greek and Roman times, it was believed that lupines destroyed the soil, wolfing the nourishment from the earth. Because of this, the plant was named after the wolf, called *lupus* in Latin. Lupines are actually one of the plants that add nitrogen to the soil, thus improving the quality of poor soils.

DESCRIPTION: All members of the genus *Lupinus* have palmately compound leaves, the blades of which are divided into four to eight elongated leaflets, all radiating from the same point on the leafstalk. The pealike blue or white flowers of the genus

Lupinus grow at the tip of hollow stems or branches in a dense spikelike raceme. The flowers have a broad upper petal, two lateral petals, and two bottom petals. The bottom petals are joined and shaped like the prow of a boat. There are a few yellow-flowered lupine species. Lupines have ten stamens. Nine of them are joined by their filaments to form a sheath around the ovary. The tenth stamen is attached at the base of the sheath and has nothing to do with the ovary. Leaves are mostly basal, and the seed pods are flat and hairy. The different species range in size from small ones like *Lupinus lyallii*, which is only about five inches (12.5 cm) tall, to the shrublike yellow bush lupine (*Lupinus arboreus*), which can grow up to nine feet (2.7 m) tall.

HABITAT: Anywhere from dry ground to moist stream banks, from valleys to alpine elevations.

SEASON: May to August.

COMMENTS: The flat seeds of lupines were used as stage money in Roman theater. The state flower of Texas is *Lupinus subcarnosus*, known as Texas bluebonnet. The oldest known viable seeds ever found on earth were discovered in a lemming burrow in 1967. The seeds were from a species of arctic lupine and were estimated to be 10,000 years old. They germinated forty-eight hours after planting. The hard, smooth seeds are a valuable food source for a few species of birds, including Clark's nutcracker and the mountain quail. Grizzly and black bear are fond of the seeds, pods, and roots of some of the nontoxic species of lupines. Many species of lupines are toxic. As the seeds and pods of poisonous lupines form, they produce alkaloids that are fatal if eaten in large quantities.

In his typical transcendental style, Henry David Thoreau wrote: "The Lupine is now in its glory. It is the more important because it occurs in such extensive patches, even an acre or more together. . . . It paints a whole hillside with its blue, making a field, if not a meadow, as Proserpine [the Greek goddess personifying spring] might have wandered in. Its leaf was made to be covered with dewdrops. . . . Such a profusion of the heavenly, the Elysian color, as if these were the Elysian Fields. That is the value of the Lupine. The earth is blued with it. You may have passed here a fortnight ago and the field is comparatively barren. Now you come here, and these glorious redeemers appear to have flashed out here all at once. Who plants the seed of Lupines in the barren soil? Who watereth the Lupines in the field?"

MOUNTAIN BLUEBELLS
(*Mertensia longiflora*)
BORAGE FAMILY

NAME SOURCE: The genus name, *Mertensia*, commemorates the German botanist Franz Carl Mertens (1764–1831). The specific epithet, *longiflora*, is from Latin and means "long-flowered."

DESCRIPTION: A perennial, it grows up to eight inches (20 cm) tall and has one to several leafy stems, each topped by a drooping head of nodding flowers. The dark blue petals of each flower are joined for most of their length, forming a tube. The leathery, bluish leaves on the stem are three-fourths to three inches (2–7.5 cm) long and less than half as broad. Basal leaves also develop, but usually not until after the plant flowers.

HABITAT: Damp meadows.

SEASON: April to June.

Mountain bluebells is one of the first flowers to bloom in the spring after the snow melts.

COMMENTS: *Mertensia ciliata* grows up to four feet (1.2 m) tall. It is browsed by deer, elk, and bear. The pika (rock rabbit) stores it for winter.

In 1859, the Englishman James Carnegie, Earl of Southesk, journeyed to the Canadian Rockies on a hunting expedition. Among his personal effects were a portable table, a camp stool, and an India rubber bath. The bath was considered a necessary comfort for a well-bred Victorian traveler. On July 7, his party was east of Edmonton, Alberta, heading toward the Rockies. He wrote in his diary: "Flowers of the gayest colour enlivened the landscape. The most common were the small tiger-lilies and the roses, and next came blue-bells and white strawberry blossoms. Sometimes acres and acres were covered with intermingled masses of the orange lily and the pendulous blue-bell, the whole of them so short of stem that the glory of the flowers combined with the rich greenness of their leaves, and it seemed as if a vast oriental carpet had been thrown upon the plain."

In her romantic style, Agnes Laut described her experiences when she visited what was then Waterton-Glacier Park in the 1920s in *Enchanted Trails of Glacier Park*. About the flowers in the Bowman Lake area, she wrote: "You see such a glory of flowers here as nowhere else in Glacier Park. There is the windflower or spring anemone with her wooly hair to protect her seedling from neuralgia in the chill off the mountain snows.... There are daisies and asters and sunflowers of every hue. There are the purple fire-flowers [fireweed], growing, the Indians say, where fires have run.... There are buttercups holding up a chalice of dew to the sun ... purple and white heathers to tear at the heartstrings of a Scotchman ... bluebells graceful of stem as a girl's throat, ringing a music only the birds hear ... columbines trembling to the touch of every breeze. There are forget-me-nots—believe me, you couldn't forget them if you tried" (Laut: No. 4 on Waterton-Glacier International Peace Park map).

FORGET-ME-NOT
(Myosotis alpestris)
BORAGE FAMILY

NAME SOURCE: The genus name, *Myosotis*, is Greek and means "mouse eared," a reference to the short pointed leaves of some species. A tale in Christian mythology accounts for the common name, forget-me-not. God named all the plants during the creation, but one small plant could never remember its name. God forgave the little flower its forgetfulness and whispered, "Forget-me-not. That shall be thy name."

DESCRIPTION: A perennial, ten to twenty-five inches (25–62 cm) tall, it has a weak, slender stem that finishes in a cluster of tiny bright-blue flowers with yellow centers. Its slender stem has oblong to lance-shaped leaves up to five inches long and covered with stiff short hairs. It usually extends along the ground for several inches before rising to the flower cluster. The pretty flowers are only about one-fourth inch (6 mm) wide.

HABITAT: Moist meadows in subalpine and alpine areas.

SEASON: June to September.

COMMENTS: In 1858–1862, the British Boundary Commission surveyed the 49th Parallel from the West Coast to the Continental Divide, which marked the official boundary between Canada and the United States. Charles Wilson, secretary of the commission, kept a diary of those four years for his sister Fanny, back in England. On July 31, 1861, their work was completed. Wilson and two other men decided to hike up to the final boundary marker that the surveyors had erected. It stands on the Continental Divide above Cameron Lake in present-day Waterton-Glacier International Peace Park. About reaching the marker, Wilson wrote: "[W]e stood on the narrow shoulder beside the cairn of stones which marked the end of our labours.... The view from this point was very fine, precipices and peaks, glaciers and rocks all massed together ... Fancy our delight at finding on a grassy spot, close to a huge bank of snow the dear old 'Forget-me-not' which carried our thoughts far away from the wild mountains to many a pleasant spring day of 'Auld lang syne' in 'merrie England'; I send you some which I gathered right on the summit" (Wilson: No. 5 on Waterton-Glacier International Peace Park map).

John Muir, one of America's greatest naturalists, related an episode that involved the forget-me-not. While exploring some gold-laced stream banks in southeast Alaska, he met "an interesting French Canadian, who ... invited me to accompany him to his gold mine ... we arrived at the cabin about the middle of the afternoon. Before entering it he ... show[ed] me his favorite flower, a blue forget-me-not, a specimen of which he found within a few rods of the cabin."

In 1914, Lawrence Burpee wrote his travelogue-style *Among the Canadian Alps*, recording the splendor of the Canadian Rockies. Northeast of Mt. Robson, the highest peak in those mountains, is Moose Pass in Jasper National Park, resplendent with wildflowers when Burpee was there. He wrote: "Imagine a great bowl of dark rock relieved here and there with patches of fresh snow, and at the foot of this bowl a soft emerald carpet, the green almost hidden by glowing patches of flowers, asters and arbutus and harebell, purple and white heather, lady's tresses and columbine, moss campion, the twin flower and the forget-me-not. Think of it, you who treasure a little patch of forget-me-nots in your garden, think of walking your horse reverently through an acre of forget-me-nots, growing so thickly that the blue of them could be seen long before one reached the place where they grew, so thickly that one was compelled to the sacrilege of treading down thousands of blossoms as we crossed the meadow" (Burpee: No. 4 on Jasper National Park map).

PENSTEMON
(*Penstemon*)
FIGWORT FAMILY

More than 100 species of the genus Penstemon are found in the Rocky Mountain area. It is often difficult to make a positive identification of penstemons, but the flowers are very distinctive and hard to confuse with other flowers. The description given is a general one for the genus. Penstemons are found almost entirely in North America.

OTHER NAMES: Beard-tongue.

NAME SOURCE: The genus name, *Penstemon*, is from the Greek words *pente*, meaning "five," and *stemon*, meaning "stamen," a reference to the flower's five stamens, one of which is sterile.

DESCRIPTION: The showy flower of members of the genus *Penstemon* is very distinctive. The flower's petals are fused, forming a tube. The part of the corolla called the limb is two-lipped. The upper lip is curved upward, and the lower lip is curved down and outward. The shape of the lower lip forms a landing place for nectar-seeking pollinators of the flower. All penstemons have five stamens, of which four are fertile. The fifth stamen is sterile and is usually covered with golden-colored hair, giving it the appearance of a bearded tongue. The palate of many penstemons is covered with short hairs. Penstemons are found in a wide variety of colors, including white, yellow, pale lavender, deep blue, purple, and red. Members of the genus range in size from the lavender-flowered mat penstemon (*Penstemon caespitosus*), which grows to only one to two inches (2.5–5 cm) tall and forms a dense creeping mat to Lyall's beard-tongue (*Penstemon lyallii*), which has blue flowers and can grow to three feet (90 cm) tall. There are only a few white-flowered species of *Penstemon*. One of them is hot rock penstemon (*Penstemon deustus*), which has an unpleasant-smelling flower.

HABITAT: Most grow in moderately dry, somewhat sandy soils or on rocky ridges to alpine elevations.

SEASON: May to August.

COMMENTS: *Penstemon* is the largest genus in the Figwort Family. Ground squirrels eat the seeds of many of its species. Some of the red-flowered species lack the well-differentiated landing platform of most members of the genus and have adapted their flower radically for pollination by hummingbirds.

Frank Morris wrote an article in 1926 for the magazine *Canadian Field-Naturalist* about his first visit to Jasper National Park the previous summer. As a botanist, his excitement about the flowers and plants he encountered permeates the article. He spent two days exploring the area around Mt. Edith Cavell. Morris wrote: "Both days were filled to the brim with excitement. The colouring of the flowers was a perfect miracle, no less than their lavish profusion. The wet gravel beds of the delta were aflame with mountain Fireweed. . . . Almost on the edge of the glacier, in the midst of icy streams, lay a little island entirely covered with plants of Western Castilleia—the Indian Paint-brush. . . . On the steep rock slide below the precipice, we found thickets of beautiful white-flowered Mountain Rhododendron . . . and big drooping sprays of violet Beard Tongue [*Penstemon*]. Other finds just as interesting, if not so obvious . . . served to make of this rocky staircase on the mountain-side a veritable Jacob's ladder from earth to heaven for the botanist to run up and down" (Morris: No. 3 on Jasper National Park map).

SELFHEAL
(*Prunella vulgaris*)
MINT FAMILY

OTHER NAMES: Heal-all.

NAME SOURCE: The genus name, *Prunella*, is from the Latin word *prunum*, meaning "purple," a reference to the plant's purple flowers. The specific epithet, *vulgaris*, means "common."

DESCRIPTION: A low-growing perennial, to six inches (15 cm) tall, it has squarish stems, opposite leaves, and a short, dense, leafy spike of small purplish-blue flowers at the top. The flowers, about three-eighths inch (9 mm) long, are crowded into a short terminal spike. Each tiny flower has two lips. The upper lip is arched, the lower one divided into three parts.

HABITAT: Wet places by brooks and streams.

SEASON: May to July.

COMMENTS: Selfheal, a weed introduced to this continent from Europe, was once highly prized for its healing qualities.

The Yoho Valley in Canada's Yoho National Park is a diverse and spectacular area. In *Among the Canadian Alps*, Lawrence Burpee described the valley and its environment: "It is impossible to give more than a mere impression of the charms of this delightful valley. It would indeed be difficult to find anywhere else a more perfect grouping of the elements of Rocky Mountain scenery, great peaks and glaciers, stately forests and meadows carpeted with wild-flowers, rushing streams, lakes of the most exquisite colouring, and a group of waterfalls as varied in character as they are all strikingly beautiful" (Burpee: No. 2 on Kootenay-Yoho National Park map).

The delicate flowers of mountain bells (*Stenanthium occidentale*).

Brown Flowers

IT WAS A GREAT THING TO LEARN ABOUT THE FLOWERS AT AND ABOVE THE SNOW LINE AND TO SEE THEM HUSTLE FORTH AS SOON AS THE SNOW LEFT, FOR THEY HAVE A VERY SHORT SPAN OF TIME IN WHICH TO SHOOT, BUD, AND BLOSSOM.

–Wilderness explorer
Albert Sperry, 1894

WILD GINGER
(*Asarum caudatum*)
BIRTHWORT FAMILY

NAME SOURCE: The specific epithet, *caudatum*, means "having a tail," a reference to the long tails on the sepal. The common name, ginger, is derived from the Sanskrit word *srngaverem*, which means "horn body" and describes the plant's pointed rhizome.

DESCRIPTION: A creeping perennial, it displays a pair of fairly large, heart-shaped, shiny leaves growing on hair-covered stems, three to seven inches (7.5–18 cm) tall. The brown-purplish to yellowish or greenish flower is often hidden beneath the leaves. The heart-shaped leaves grow in pairs and are two to six inches (5–15 cm) wide and up to four inches (10 cm) long. There are a few fine hairs on the leaves. Wild ginger grows from a rhizome that creeps along just under the surface of the ground and can form dense patches. The solitary flower under each pair of leaves grows on a short stem that barely lifts it above the ground. The odd looking, bell-like flower is one and one-half to five inches (3.8–12.5 cm) wide, with no petals. The three triangular-shaped sepals, one to three and one-half inches (2.5–8.5 cm) long, taper to slender elongated tips. The flower has twelve stamens.

HABITAT: Moist shady woods, often where there is thick leaf mold.

The brown-purplish flower of wild ginger
is often hidden under the large heart-shaped leaves.

SEASON: April to July.

COMMENTS: Wild ginger was highly regarded as a medicinal plant to Native Americans. Research on the rhizomes has shown they contain antibiotic substances that are active against pus-forming bacteria. The dried and grated root can be used as a substitute for commercial ginger. The crushed leaves and rhizomes give off a strong odor.

At the end of June 1806, the Lewis and Clark Expedition was headed back to the East Coast after reaching the Pacific Ocean the year before, returning by way of Lolo Pass on the Idaho–Montana border. At the time, Captain Clark was attending to a man in his party who had an injured leg. In his journal on June 27, 1806, Clark wrote: "Jo. Potts leg which had been much Swelled and inflaimed for several days is much better this evening and givs him but little pain. We applied the pounded root and leaves of wild ginger from which he found great relief."

SPOTTED CORALROOT
(*Corallorhiza maculata*)

ORCHID FAMILY

OTHER NAMES: Mottled coralroot.

NAME SOURCE: The genus name, *Corallorhiza*, is Greek and refers to the plant's coral-like rhizome. The rhizome is repeatedly divided into short, thick, coral-like fibers. The specific epithet, *maculata*, is Latin and means "spotted," a reference to the purplish spots on the lip of the flower.

DESCRIPTION: This plant grows from six to thirty-two inches (15–80 cm) tall with erect, unbranched, nearly leafless, pinkish-purple stems that terminate in a loose raceme of small reddish-brown flowers. The raceme of flowers is four to eight inches (10–20 cm) long. Each flower in the raceme is only about one-half inch (1.3 cm) long and is distinguished by the purple-spotted white lip. The lip is also about one-half inch (1.3 cm) long and nearly as wide. The unbranched stems arise in clumps, growing from a thick, tuberlike rootstock. Outstanding characteristics include the brownish-purple color, the absence of leaves, and the lack of chlorophyll.

HABITAT: In decaying humus in moist to fairly dry woods.

SEASON: May to August.

COMMENTS: Luther Burbank was an American horticulturist who produced many new varieties of plants. About orchids in general, he said: "I remember once being asked if I had ever done any work to improve orchids. I stared at the questioner for a moment or two, fumbling for a reply. And then I said, perhaps a little impatiently: 'Improve orchids? But who on earth would dream of wanting them improved?'"

PINEDROPS
(Pterospora andromedea)

WINTERGREEN FAMILY

OTHER NAMES: Giant bird's nest, Albany beech drops.

NAME SOURCE: The genus name, *Pterospora*, is from the Greek words *pteron*, meaning "wing," and *sperma*, meaning "seed." This refers to the plant's minute seeds, which have a netlike wing at one end that helps the wind to carry them to new locations.

DESCRIPTION: A plant, one to four feet (30–120 cm) tall, it usually has several leafless, unbranched, sticky, hairy, reddish-brown stems growing in a cluster. Each stem culminates in a long raceme of red to white, urn-shaped, nodding flowers. The flowers in the terminal raceme have petals about three-eighths inch (9 mm) long, joined into an urn shape. These flowers hang downward like bells, usually have ten stamens, and turn a brownish color as they age. Some narrow brown scales can be found on the lower part of the erect hairy stems. The roots form coarse irregular masses.

HABITAT: Deep humus of coniferous forests where there is an abundance of decaying plant material.

SEASON: June to August.

COMMENTS: The stems grow for one year and then remain standing as dried stalks.

MOUNTAIN BELLS
(*Stenanthium occidentale*)
LILY FAMILY

OTHER NAMES: Bronze bells.

NAME SOURCE: The genus name, *Stenanthium*, is from the Greek words *stenos*, meaning "narrow," and *anthos*, meaning "flower," a reference to the flower's narrow petals and sepals. The specific epithet, occidentale, means "Western."

DESCRIPTION: A plant with basal leaves from which grows a delicate stem, four to twenty inches (10–50 cm) tall, it is topped by several small, bell-shaped, greenish-purple flowers that nod gracefully. The bell-shaped flowers at the top of the delicate stem are about three-fourths inch (2 cm) long. Each of the flower's six narrow petal-like segments is curved back at the tip. Its several narrow, basal leaves are from four to twelve inches (10–30 cm) long.

HABITAT: Moist wooded slopes and along shady mountain streams.

SEASON: June to August.

COMMENTS: Its pretty bell-shaped flowers are very fragrant. There are only five species of the genus *Stenanthium* in the world, and four of them are found in North America.

Glossary

ALTERNATE—leaves that arise singly along the stem

ANNUAL—a plant that has a life cycle that is completed in one year or season

ANTHER—the pollen-bearing part of the stamen

AXIL—the angle between a leaf and its stem

BASAL—leaves at the base of a plant

BLADE—the flat or expanded part of a leaf

BRACT—a small modified leaf or leaves that when present are found near the base of a flower or flower cluster

BROWSE—the tender twigs, leaves, and shoots that animals eat

BUD—an undeveloped flower or leafy shoot

BULB—an enlarged underground leaf bud with fleshy scales; for food storage, such as garlic and onions

CALYX—the collective term for the sepals of a flower, which are generally green

CAPSULE—a dry seed vessel that opens at maturity

CHLOROPHYLL—the green pigment of plants

COMPOUND LEAF—a leaf that has the blade divided into leaflets

CONICAL—cone shaped

CORM—an enlarged, solid, fleshy base of a stem that is underground and looks like a bulb

COROLLA—the collective term for the petals of a flower

DECIDUOUS—plants that drop their leaves seasonally

DIOECIOUS—flowers that are either male or female

DISK FLOWER—the tiny tubular flowers in the central part of the floral head in many members of the Composite Family

DISSECTED—deeply divided into smaller parts

ELLIPTIC—narrowly ovate in shape

EVERGREEN—having green leaves throughout the winter

FILAMENT—the stamen's stalk

FRUIT—the seed-bearing structure of a plant

HERBACEOUS—pertaining to herbs or to a plant that is not woody

INFLORESCENCE—the flower cluster of a plant

INVOLUCRE—a set of bracts that occurs beneath an inflorescence

LANCEOLATE—lance shaped; broadest near the base and narrowing gradually to the tip

LEAFLET—one of the leaflike segments of a compound leaf

LIP—the lower petal or petals of a two-lobed corolla, as in many members of the Orchid Family

LOBE—indented on the margins, with each indentation halfway or less to the center and the outer points usually blunt or rounded

NUTLET—a small, hard, thick-walled fruit that usually has only one seed on the inside

OB—a Greek prefix that means "in reverse direction"

OBLONG—much longer than broad, with parallel sides

OPPOSITE—having two leaves originating at the same place on opposite sides of the stem

OVARY—the fertile portion of the pistil

OVATE—egg shaped, being broadest below the middle

PALATE—the raised part of the lower part of the corolla that partly or entirely closes the throat

PALMATE—leaves that are arranged like the outspread fingers of a hand

PAPPUS—a modified calyx that crowns the ovary of Composite Family flowers

PARASITE—a plant that derives its nourishment from another living plant

PERENNIAL—a plant that lives and reproduces for more than two years

PERFECT—a bisexual flower

PINNATE—a compound leaf arranged like a feather, in which the smaller leaflets appear on opposite sides of a common central stalk

PETAL—the part of the flower, usually colored, that is the basic unit of the corolla

PISTIL—the ovule-bearing organ of a flower, composed of the ovary, stigma, and style

POME—a fruit with a core, such as an apple

RACEME—an elongated flower cluster on which each flower has its own flower stalk with the lower flowers usually blooming first

RAY FLOWER—one of the two types of flowers that make up the flower head of many members of the Composite Family; the marginal flowers of the flower head, with each flower resembling a single petal, an example being the white petals of the daisy

RHIZOME—a stem that creeps underground

ROOTSTALK OR ROOTSTOCK—an underground rootlike stem

ROSETTE—a circular cluster of leaves usually growing at the base of a plant

RUNNER—a slender stolon

SCALE—thin, flat, small, often translucent leaflike structures

SEPAL—the basic unit of the calyx, which resembles a petal; generally green, though sometimes colored

SHEATH—a tubular envelope that is the lower part of the leaf that surrounds the stem in grasses

SHRUB—a woody plant that usually branches at ground level with more than one main axis

SPADIX—the fleshy axis of a spike

SPATHE—a large, usually solitary bract that often encloses a spadix or other kind of inflorescence

SPIKE—an elongated flower cluster with stalkless flowers

SPINE—a modified stem or branch that is sharply pointed and stiff

STAMEN—the pollen-bearing part of a flower, made up of a filament topped by a pollen-bearing anther; usually several appear in each flower

STIGMA—the part of the pistil that receives the pollen during pollination

STOLON—a prostrate, creeping stem on the ground's surface

STYLE—the narrowed portion of the pistil that connects the stigma to the ovary

SUCCULENT—thickly fleshy

TAPROOT—a stout main root that descends vertically into the ground

TERMINAL—at the tip of a stem

TUBER—a thick underground stem, branch, or root that stores food

UMBEL—a generally flat-topped flower cluster in which all the flower stalks arise from the same point

WHORL—three or more leaves growing from the same point on the stem, usually in a circle

Bibliography

Adair, James. *History of the American Indian.* London: E. and C. Dilly, 1775.

Amery, Leopold. "A Month in the Canadian Rockies." *Canadian Alpine Journal* (May, 1930).

Bartlet, Richard. *Nature's Yellowstone.* Albuquerque: University of New Mexico Press, 1974.

Bemis, Katherine, and Mathilde Holtz. *Glacier National Park: Its Trails and Treasures.* New York: George H. Doran Co., 1917.

Bird, Isabella. *A Lady's Life in the Rocky Mountains.* London: John Murray, 1879.

Bonney, Oren H., and Lorraine Bonney. *Battle Drums and Geysers.* Chicago: Sage Books, 1978.

Brooks, Paul. *Speaking for Nature.* Boston: Houghton Mifflin Co., 1980.

Brown, Stewardson. *Alpine Flora of the Canadian Rocky Mountains.* New York and London: G. P. Putnam's Sons, 1907.

Buchholz, C. W. *Man in Glacier.* West Glacier, Mont.: Glacier Natural History Association, 1976.

_____. *Rocky Mountain National Park: A History.* Boulder: Colorado Associated University Press, 1983.

Burbank, Luther, with Wilbur Hall. *The Harvest of the Years.* Boston and New York: Houghton Mifflin Co., 1927.

Burpee, Lawrence. *Among the Canadian Alps.* New York: John Lane Co., 1914.

Burroughs, John. *Camping and Tramping with President Roosevelt.* Boston: Houghton Mifflin Co., 1907.

_____. *Riverby.* Boston and New York: Houghton Mifflin Co., 1896.

_____. *Signs and Seasons.* Boston and New York: Houghton Mifflin Co., 1886.

Butters, Frederick King. "Flora of the Glacier District." *Canadian Alpine Journal* (1932): 139–147.

Cartwright, Paul R. "Meriwether Lewis: Naturalist." *Oregon Historical Quarterly* (1968).

Cheadle, W. B. *Cheadle's Journal of Trip Across Canada: 1862–1863.* Ottawa: Graphic Publications, 1931.

Chittenden, H. M. *H. M. Chittenden: A Western Epic.* Edited by Bruce LeRoy. Seattle: Washington State Historical Society, 1961.

_____. *Yellowstone National Park: Historical and Descriptive.* Stanford, Calif: Stanford University Press, 1895.

Clark, Lewis J. *Wildflowers of British Columbia.* Sidney, British Columbia: Gray's Publishing, 1973.

_____. *Wildflowers of Marsh and Waterway.* Sidney, British Columbia: Gray's Publishing, 1974.

_____. *Wildflowers of the Mountains.* Sidney, British Columbia: Gray's Publishing, 1975.

Clute, Willard Nelson. *The Common Names of Plants and Their Meanings.* Indianapolis, Ind.: W. N. Clute and Co., 1931.

Coleman, A. P. *The Canadian Rockies: New and Old Trails.* London: Charles Scribner, 1911.

Collie, J. Norman, and Hugh Stutfield. *Climbs and Explorations in the Canadian Rockies.* London: Green and Co., 1903.

Cox, Ross. *Adventures on the Columbia River.* London: Henry Colburn and Richard Bentley, 1831.

Craighead, John, Frank Craighead, and Ray Davis. *Field Guide to Rocky Mountain Wildflowers.* Boston: Houghton Mifflin Co., 1963.

DeSmet, Pierre-Jean. *Life, Letters, and Travels of Father Pierre-Jean DeSmet.* Edited by H. M. Chittenden, New York: Francis Harper, 1905.

Dickinson, Anna E. *A Ragged Register (of People, Places, and Opinions).* New York: Harper and Brothers, 1879.

Douglas, David. *Journal Kept by David Douglas During His Travels in North America: 1823–1827.* London: Royal Horticultural Society, 1914.

_____. *Douglas of the Forests.* Edited by John Davies. Seattle: University of Washington Press, 1980.

Dunraven, Earl of. *Canadian Nights.* London: Smith, Elder, and Co., 1914.

_____. *The Great Divide.* London: Chatto and Windus, 1876.

Durant, Mary. *Who Named the Daisy? Who Named the Rose?* New York: Dodd, Mead, 1976, Congdon and Weed, 1983.

Fleming, Sir Sanford. *A Summer Tour Between Old and New Westminster.* London: Sampson Low, Marston, Searle, and Rivington, 1884.

_____. *Canadian Pacific Railway: Report of Progress on the Exploration and Surveys Up to January 1874.* Ottawa: Government Printing Bureau, 1876.

_____. "Memories of the Mountains." *Canadian Alpine Journal* I (2): 10–33.

Flory, J. S. *Thrilling Echoes from the Wild Frontier.* Chicago: Rhodes and McClure Publishing Co., 1893.

Folsom, David. *The Folsom-Cook Exploration of the Upper Yellowstone in the Year 1869.* St. Paul, Minn.: H. L. Collins Printers, 1894.

Fraser, Ester. *The Canadian Rockies: Early Travels and Explorations.* Edmonton, Alberta: Hurtig, 1969.

Fraser, Simon. *Letters and Journals.* Toronto: Macmillan, 1960.

Fuller, Harlin M., and LeRoy Hafen. *The Journal of Captain John R. Bell.* Glendale, Calif.: Arthur H. Clark Co., 1973.

Graham, Stephen. *Tramping with a Poet in the Rockies.* New York: D. Appleton, 1922.

Grant, George Munro. *Ocean to Ocean.* London: Sampson Low, Marston, Searle, and Rivington, 1873.

Green, William S. *Among the Selkirk Glaciers.* London and New York: Macmillan, 1890.

Grinnell, George Bird. *Beyond the Old Frontier.* New York: Charles Scribner, 1913.

_____. *The Passing of the Great West: Selected Papers of George Bird Grinnell.* Norman, Okla.: University of Oklahoma Press, 1985.

_____. *Trails of the Pathfinders.* New York: C. Scribner's Sons, 1911.

_____. "The Crown of the Continent." *Century* magazine (1901): 660–672.

Harmon, Bryon. *Great Days in the Rockies.* Toronto: Oxford University Press, 1978.

Hart, Jeff. Montana: *Native Plants and Early Peoples.* Helena, Mont.: Montana Historical Society and Montana Bicentennial Administration, 1976.

Henry, Alexander, and David Thompson. *The Manuscript Journals of Alexander Henry, Fur Traveler of the Northwest Company, and of David Thompson, Official Geographer and Explorer of the Same Company, 1799–1814.* Edited by Elliott Coues. Minneapolis, Minn.: Ross and Haines, 1965.

Hill, Douglas. *The Opening of the Canadian West.* London: Heinemann, 1967.

Hitchcock, Leo, and Arthur Cronquist. *Flora of the Pacific Northwest.* Seattle and London: University of Washington Press, 1973.

Hornaday, William T. *Camp-Fires in the Canadian Rockies.* New York: C. Scribner's Sons, 1906.

Jackson, William Henry. *The Diaries of William Henry Jackson.* Edited by LeRoy Hafen and Ann Hafen. Glendale, Calif.: Arthur H. Clark Co., 1959.

_____. *Time Exposure: The Autobiography of William Henry Jackson.* New York: G. P. Putnam's Sons, 1940.

James, Edwin. *Account of an Expedition from Pittsburgh to the Rocky Mountains.* Philadelphia: Atlas, 1823.

Kain, Conrad. *Where the Clouds Can Go.* New York: American Alpine Club, 1935.

Kane, Paul. *Wanderings of an Artist Among the Indians of North America.* London: Longman, Brown, Green, Longmans, and Roberts, 1859.

Langford, Nathaniel Pitt. *The Discovery of Yellowstone Park.* St. Paul, Minn.: J. E. Haynes, 1892.

Laut, Agnes. *Enchanted Trails of Glacier Park.* New York: Robert M. McBride, 1926.

Leopold, Aldo. *A Sand County Almanac.* New York: Oxford University Press, 1949.

Lewis, Meriwether, and William Clark. *The History of the Expedition under the Command of Lewis and Clark.* Edited by Elliott Coues. New York: F. P. Harper, 1893.

_____. *The Journals of Lewis and Clark.* Edited by Bernard DeVoto. Boston: Houghton Mifflin Co., 1953.

Longstaff, Thomas. *This My Voyage.* London: John Murray, 1950.

Ludlow, William. *Exploring Nature's Sanctuary: Captain William Ludlow's Report of a Reconnaissance from Carrol, Montana Territory on the Upper Missouri to the Yellowstone National Park and Return Made in the Summer of 1875.* Introduction by Paul K. Walker. Washington D.C.: Historical Division, Office of Administrative Services, Office of the Chief of Engineers, 1985.

MacFadden, F. A. "British Columbia: The Bryologist's Paradise." *Bryologist* (1926): 56–61.

_____. "A Trip to Tonquin Valley." *Bryologist* (1927): 65–71.

Macoun, John. *Autobiography of John Macoun.* Ottawa: Field Naturalists' Club, 1922.

Macoun, J. M., and M. O. Malte. "Flora of Canada." *Canada Geological Survey, Biological Series* 6 (1917): 1–14.

Marshall, Robert. *Alaska Wilderness: Exploring the Central Brooks Range.* Los Angeles and London: University of California Press, 1970.

Martin, Alexander, et al. *American Wildlife and Plants.* New York: Dover Publications, 1961.

Maximilian, Prince of Wied-Neuwied. *Travels in the Interior of North America.* London: Ackermann and Co., 1843.

McCowan, Don. *A Naturalist in Canada.* Toronto: Macmillan, 1941.

McDougall, John. *Pathfinding on Plain and Prairie.* Toronto: William Brigs, 1898.

McKelvey, Susan Delano. *Botanical Exploration of the Trans-Mississippi West: 1790–1850.* Jamaica Plain, Mass.: Arnold Arboretum of Harvard University Press, 1955.

Meehan, Thomas. *The Native Flowers and Plants of the United States in Their Botanical, Horticultural, and Popular Aspects.* Boston: L. Prang and Co., 1880.

Mills, Enos. *Adventures of a Nature Guide.* Garden City, N.Y.: Doubleday, Page, 1920.

_____. *The Rocky Mountain Wonderland.* Boston: Houghton Mifflin Co., 1915.

_____. *Spell of the Rockies.* Boston: Houghton Mifflin Co., 1911.

_____. *The Story of Early Estes Park.* Denver, Colo.: Outdoor Life Publishing Co., 1917.

_____. *Your National Parks.* Boston and New York: Houghton Mifflin Co., 1917.

Milton, Viscount, and W. B. Cheadle. *The North-West Passage by Land.* London: Cassell, Peter, and Galpin, 1865.

Moberly, Walter. *The Rocks and Rivers of British Columbia.* London: H. Blacklock and Co., 1885.

Moomaw, Jack C. *Recollections of a Rocky Mountain Ranger.* Longmont, Colo.: Times-Call Publishing Co., 1963.

Morris, Frank. "Nature Lovers at Jasper." *Canadian Field-Naturalist* February (1926): 26–31.

Muir, John. *Letters to a Friend: Written to Mrs. Ezra S. Carr, 1866–1879.* Dunwoody, Ga.: N. A. Berg, 1915.

_____. *Our National Parks.* Boston and New York: Houghton Mifflin Co., 1901.

_____. *Travels in Alaska.* Boston: Houghton Mifflin Co., 1915.

Nelson, Ruth A. *Plants of Rocky Mountain National Park.* Boulder, Colo.: Colorado Association, 1970.

Outram, James. *In the Heart of the Canadian Rockies.* London and New York: Macmillan, 1905.

Palliser, John. *The Papers of the Palliser Expedition.* Edited by Irene Spry. Toronto: Macmillan, 1963.

_____. *Solitary Rambles and Adventures of a Hunter in the Prairies.* London: 1853.

Palmer, Howard. *Mountaineering and Exploration in the Selkirks: A Record of Pioneer Work Among the Canadian Alps: 1908–1912.* New York and London: G. P. Putnam's Sons, 1914.

Parsons, Frances Theodora. *According to the Seasons.* New York: C. Scribner's Sons, 1894.

Phillips Walter J., and Frederick Niven. *Colour in the Canadian Rockies.* Toronto: Thomas Nelson and Sons Ltd., 1937.

Porsild, A. E. *Rocky Mountain Wildflowers.* Ottawa: National Museum of Natural Sciences and National Museums of Canada and Parks Canada, 1974.

Rawlings, Marjorie Kinnan. *Cross Creek.* New York: Charles Scribner's Sons, 1942.

Remington, Frederick. *Pony Tracks.* New York: Harper and Brothers, 1895.

Rinehart, Mary. *Tenting To-Night.* Boston: Houghton Mifflin Co., 1918.

_____. *Through Glacier Park in 1915.* New York: P. F. Collier and Son, 1916.

Robinson, Reverend J. J. "Vermillion Pass Camp, 1912." *Canadian Alpine Journal* 5 (1912): 100–108.

Rodgers, Andres Denny. *John Merle Coulter: Missionary in Science.* Princeton, N.J.: Princeton University Press, 1944.

Ross, Alexander. *Adventures of the First Settlers on the Columbia River.* London: Smith, Elder and Co., 1849.

Russell, Osborne. *Journal of a Trapper: 1834–1843.* Boise, Id.: Syms-York, 1921.

Sage, Rufus B. *Scenes in the Rocky Mountains.* Philadelphia: Carey and Hart, 1846.

Schaffer, Mary. *Old Indian Trails.* New York and London: G. P. Putnam's Sons, 1911.

Schullery, Paul. *Old Yellowstone Days.* Boulder, Colo.: Colorado University Associated Press, 1979.

Simpson, Sir George. *Narrative of a Journey Round the World During the Years 1841 and 1842.* London: Henry Colburn, 1847.

Southesk, Earl of (James Carnegie). *Saskatchewan and the Rocky Mountains: A Diary and Narrative of Travel, Sport, and Adventure, During a Journey Through the Hudson's Bay Company's Territories in 1859 and 1860.* Edinburgh: Edmonston and Douglas, 1875.

Sperry, Albert. *Avalanche.* Boston: Christopher Publishing House, 1938.

Strahorn, Carrie Adell. *Fifteen Thousand Miles by Stage.* New York: G. P. Putnam's Sons, 1915.

Strong, General W. E. *A Trip to Yellowstone National Park in July, August, and September, 1875.* Tulsa: University of Oklahoma Press, 1968.

Thompson, David. *David Thompson: Travels in North America, 1784–1812.* Edited by Victor G. Hopwood. Toronto: Macmillan, 1971.

Thompson, Margaret. *High Trails of Glacier National Park.* Caldwell, Id.: Caxton Printer, 1936.

Thoreau, Henry David. *Walden.* Edited by J. Lyndon Shanley. Princeton, N.J.: University of Princeton Press, 1971.

Thorington, J. Monroe. *The Glittering Mountains of Canada.* Philadelphia: John W. Lea, 1925.

Toll, Roger W. *Mountaineering in the Rocky Mountain National Park.* Washington, D.C.: Government Printing Office, 1919.

Wheeler, A. O. "Official Report of 1909 Camp." *Canadian Alpine Journal* 5: 100–108.

Wheeler, Walter. *The Selkirk Range.* Ottawa: Government Printing Bureau, 1905.

Wilcox, Walter. *The Rockies of Canada.* New York and London: G. P. Putnam's Sons, 1909.

Williams, M. B. *Through the Heart of the Rockies and Selkirks.* Ottawa: Ministry of the Interior, 1929.

Willy, John. "Five Days on Horseback in Rocky Mountain National Park." *Hotel Monthly* October (1916): 40–53.

Wilson, Charles. *Mapping the Frontier: Charles Wilson's Diary of the Survey of the 49th Parallel: 1858–1862.* Edited by George F. G. Stanley. Seattle: University of Washington Press, 1970.

Wilson, Thomas E. *Trail Blazer of the Canadian Rockies.* Edited by Hugh A. Dempsey. Calgary: Glenbow-Alberta Institute, 1972.

Index

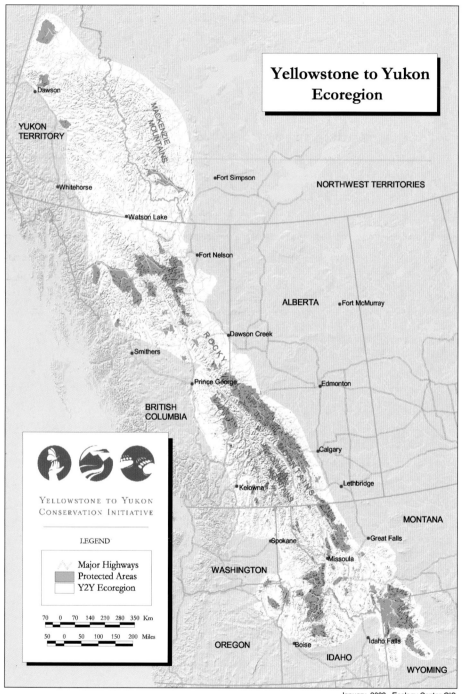

Yellowstone to Yukon
Ecoregion

YELLOWSTONE TO YUKON
CONSERVATION INITIATIVE

LEGEND

Major Highways
Protected Areas
Y2Y Ecoregion

70   0   70 140 210 280 350 Km
50   0   50 100 150 200 Miles

January, 2002 Ecology Center GIS

Yellowstone to Yukon
Conservation Initiative

All of the photographs in this book were taken within the Yellowstone to Yukon ecoregion, one of the world's most celebrated mountain landscapes. The Yellowstone to Yukon Conservation Initiative, a network of more than 300 organizations and conservation-minded individuals, is working to ensure that the region's renowned wilderness, wildlife, native plants, and natural processes continue to function as an interconnected web of life, capable of supporting all of the natural and human communities that reside within it. For more information, write to Yellowstone to Yukon, 710 9th Street, Studio B, Canmore, Alberta, Canada T1W 2V7, or visit www.y2y.net.

ABOUT THE AUTHOR

Jerry Pavia has lived in Bonners Ferry, Idaho, for the more than 25 years. He worked in the timber industry for 11 years before pursuing a career in photography. From 1995 to 2002, Jerry served as Chairman of the Board of Directors for the Idaho Conservation League, Idaho's largest environmental organization. He currently serves on the board for the Yellowstone to Yukon Conservation Initiative.

Jerry has been the sole or principal photographer of 12 books, including *Beyond the Rose Garden*, *Rooted in the Spirit*, *Yosemite National Park*, and *Yellowstone National Park*. His work appears regularly in national magazines, calendars, and greeting cards. He has had shows of his images in New York, Seattle, and Los Angeles. An avid outdoor enthusiast, Jerry has hiked and backpacked in the American and Canadian West since 1972. His other great enjoyments in life are contra dancing and working to protect the environment for future generations. *Rocky Mountain Wildflowers* is his first book as both writer and photographer.